FOREFRONT

THE CULTURE OF SHOP WINDOW DESIGN

Shonquis Moreno et al.

FRAME PUBLISHERS, AMSTERDAM
BIRKHÄUSER – PUBLISHERS FOR ARCHITECTURE, BASEL · BOSTON · BERLIN

CONTENTS

'he

Ducks, Dior and Dolly

Text by SHONQUIS MORENO
Photography by ARI MESA

NEW YORK — Born with a lisp into what he respectfully calls a 'family of lunatics', Simon Doonan blossomed in a suburban British household that included a lobotomized grandmother, a blind aunt living in the attic and an uncle with paranoid schizophrenia. By age ten, he knew he was a pouf. Today, Doonan's cheeky authenticity – in the form of window display for luxury department store Barneys – has become a New York City landmark. 'Doonan was instrumental in shifting the image of Barneys,' says Joseph Weishar, professor of display and exhibit design at New York's Fashion Institute of Technology. 'The image that he's projected has come out clearer than anything that the store has said about itself.'

Lisp gone, 52-year-old Doonan is aging handsomely. A larger-than-life character the size of a Royal Ascot jockey, for three decades he has created dioramas that occasionally cause a shriek to go up from the pavement. Calling himself a freak, as well as infantile and *outré*, Doonan peppers his speech with British slang like naff, wally and poncy, while using the flamboyant constructions of an urban queen – if it's not 'ultra-groovy', it's

Continued on page 156

Practical Magic

By SHONQUIS MORENO
Photography by JEREMY CHU

BOSTON — Over 200 years ago, Shreve, Crump & Low opened its doors to Boston. Although today the jeweller is the oldest retail store in America, it presents a fresh face, simultaneously nostalgic and modern: the result of Visual Display Director Lucy-Ann Bouwman's finely crafted and effortlessly imagined window design.

Like a collector assembling a cabinet of curiosities, Bouwman composes uncommon dioramas using common objects: eggs, children's building blocks, coloured pencils, even grass and moss. 'She's imaginative and off-the-beaten-path,' says retail expert Martin Pegler, who taught Bouwman for a year at New York City's Fashion Institute of Technology and has included her work in books he has authored since. 'She uses materials that are mundane, trite, ordinary – but makes them different, creative.'

This past spring, Bouwman dressed Shreve's windows in silk to create a series of jewel-box gardens. In these pastoral scenes, cut-crystal goblets and decanters hovered midair like dragonflies; foam floral spheres covered with moss and straw were crowned with bracelets and necklaces as if to suggest plump, jewel-eyed sheep; and each 'sky' was filled with a miniature Tord Boontje-designed chandelier – a frothy, light-filled tangle of cut-metal flowers. Bouwman gives the window a secret life. Her scenes feel conjured but not contrived: It's easy to imagine that just beyond the sill lies a rolling landscape of lollipop trees and ponds brimming with clotted cream – passers-by are granted a glimpse of fairyland. 'I don't want the window displays to look traditional,' says Bouwman. 'A great window should stop us from just hurrying

Continued on page 172

The Thre[e] seco[nd] Rule

By SHONQUIS MORENO
Photography by
RICKY ZEHAVI
& JOHN CORDES

NEW YORK — Entrance[s] Bergdorf Goodman's display win[dows] are through a series of secret d[oors] hidden in the rococo walls of the [st] interior. The Fifth Avenue win[dow] for instance, open into the jew[elry] department. Being inside [win]dows, installing displays, com[...] posure to and protection from street. The Fifth Avenue wind[ows] look out at a pageant of fashionis[tas] and tourists, while 57th Street has view of the cross-town bus and 58[th] Street supports residential traffic grannies with cotton-candy hair [...] crocodile handbags, guests of Plaza Hotel. It is in a cluttered wo[rk]shop on Bergdorf's eighth floor that the store's window displays are co[n]ceived. At various times a visitor mig[ht] find the labyrinthine rooms of the [Vi]sual Department crammed with st[...] of Mylar, pink housing insulation, m[at]tresses and metal flashing, curl[...]

Continued on page 16

Team Spirit

By REMI ABBAS

LONDON — Since the dawn of the twentieth century, Selfridges has been at the forefront of British department-store shopping. Occupying a block nestled at the top end of London's Oxford Street, it holds a majestic place within the imagination of the consumer. Famed for its explorative window design, Selfridges specializes in windows that extend beyond the physical premises of the store. These windows generate news, bridging the gap between commerce and culture through an ongoing engagement with the artistic and social pursuits that bear the mark of culture.

To ensure a high level of creativity, Selfridges relies on a nonsystematic strategy for window design. The store's Inhouse 3D Creative Team and Creative Direction Department develop themes, but they also draw upon other avenues to infuse their work with originality. After hatching a collective idea, they commission a carefully selected individual or organ-

Continued on page 52

Theater of Sales

By CHRIS SCOTT
Photography by
STÉPHANE MURATET

PARIS — The name Louis Vuitton immediately brings to mind a world of luxury, class, craftsmanship and refinement. Further enhancing the firm's impeccable image are window displays beautifully and precisely executed, frequently with an amusing or unusual touch. They originate at the Paris headquarters, where Director of Merchandising Valérie Cazals and her team oversee the design of window displays for Louis Vuitton's 319 (and rising) stores worldwide. Each outlet boasts between two and 15 windows, which are changed at least six times a year: a major operation, especially in view of LV's strong brand image,

— Louis Vuitton

which is reinforced by a myriad of messages conveyed throughout the year. These are dictated largely by new products, promotions, seasons and shows, but also by numerous rules, requirements and global calendar constraints.

Having only one brand to promote allows less freedom than that enjoyed by department stores or other establishments with a variety of brands to display. Creativity at Louis Vuitton does not appear to be stifled, however, by the obvious restrictions. Above all, LV's window designers aim for clarity of communication, preferably without sending too many messages at one time. 'What do we want to talk about?' is the recurring question. 'The windows have to talk to *you*,' replies Cazals, 'and hopefully communicate on an emotional level.'

Gaston-Louis Vuitton, grandson of founder Louis Vuitton, voiced his theoretical and practical views on display

Continued on page 104

— Vinçon

On a Mission

By SARAH MARTÍN PEARSON
Photography by
LLUÍS CAPDEVILA MARTÍN

BARCELONA — A landmark in Barcelona's design culture, Vinçon is backed by a long tradition in the sale of contemporary household appliances. Infused by a sense of innovation, this family-run business is well rooted in a philosophy that draws strength from design. Only a year after Hugo Vinçon founded the company in 1934, the Amat family entered the scene; today, seven decades later, they are still at the helm. Vinçon could not have a better location: Passeig de Gràcia is a central area of the city enriched by modernist architecture. The building Vinçon occupies was once the home of Ramon Casas (1845-1899), a Catalan painter known for his gypsy themes and advertising illustrations. The first floor, currently the furniture department, enjoys direct access to one of the city's more beautiful inner courtyards with a direct view of an adjoining building, La Pedrera, a work by Antonio Gaudí.

Vinçon's focus is on design as a vehicle of communication with a conceptual basis, a creative discipline that invigorates the mind and, in so doing, lifts design to a cultural level. In short, good design has a positive influence on society. This explains why, since 1973,

Continued on page 40

Culture Club

Text by REMI ABBAS
Photography by
MICHAEL TAYLOR

LONDON — Located on the corner of Sloane Street, overlooking Knightsbridge, Harvey Nichols exudes detached class. As a premier fashion emporium, its style harks back to a golden retail era. Wreathed in an aura of affluence and exclusivity, Harvey Nichols appeals to the coterie in the know. Elitist without being inaccessible, the establishment wears a mantle of gentility that separates it from other department stores – a sense of chic clearly conveyed by the window displays. Winner of a D&AD award in 1998 for a design created in collaboration with Thomas Heatherwick, Harvey Nichols presents windows that transcend the concept of displays to become spectacles of the imagination.

Headed by Janet Wardley, the store's visual merchandising controller, the window-design team operates with little interference from the board. Wardley has been dressing display windows for over 20 years, steadily progressing through a number of retail outfits. It is at Harvey Nichols, however, that she feels she is at the apogee of window design. 'It's the freedom that you get,' she explains.

Harvey Nichols boasts longstanding relationships among staff members. Wardley, who has been there for over

Continued on page 124

— Harvey Nichols

It's the products that count

By DAVID LITTLEFIELD
Photography by
EROS BESCHI

NEW YORK, PARIS — Staring from the centre of an immaculate white wall is the skull of a water buffalo with outrageously large horns. An arresting object, it demonstrates the power of the unexpected, of the out of scale. It is so out of place as to be almost ridiculous. This is John Field's office.

Field is Gucci's window designer. He is a direct, honest, unaffected man with an exceptional eye for detail and a highly developed sense of the surreal. He is one of those designers to whom ideas seem to come naturally and inevitably. He resists theoretical interpretations of his work, which is

— Gucci

probably wise; he works too fast to pause and ask what his creations actually mean. And his stage sets are too visually rich and suggestive to be the result of purely rational thought. Field begins with the glimmer of an idea, and two weeks later the set is complete – mannequins set against a wall of candy or a background of feathers, figures accompanied by a hooded bird. He is instinctive, a man strong on impulse without being impulsive.

Field's instinctive approach is partially explained by the lack of a formal education. Having left school in Birmingham, England, at 16, he soon found himself working on window displays at Rackhams department store. Luckily, Field thrived on this unplanned career, soon leaving for London where

Continued on page 188

Material Evidence

By CHARLOTTE VAUDREY
Photography by
STEFANO PANDINI

MILAN — Most shoppers hit Milan with finely honed must-have lists, surely none of which includes the extraordinary items topping lists drawn up by Moschino window designer JoAnn Tan, a longtime resident of Italy's fashion capital. From tracking down 1500 feather butterflies – and a glue gun – to finding four and a half tonnes of red, second-hand clothing, the Art Institute of Chicago graduate is always on the alert for potential props, especially those that can be or[...]dered in bulk. 'I'll squirrel away th[e] source,' she says, 'and when an appr[o]priate theme comes up, I'll be, lik[e] turkey feathers!'

Called Hairpets, Tan's display [at] Moschino's flagship store at the ti[me] of writing comprises pouty man[ne]quins whose hair grows, Picasso-like, into lapdogs to be petted and stroked. Flipping through a gossip mag, Tan happened upon the hair, which she would later wrap around and sew to her handmade dachshund-

Continued on page 68

Speaking Sign Language

Text by KANAE HASEGAWA
Photography by
SATOSHI ASAKAWA

TOKYO — The alluring window displays of luxury-goods retailer Hermès Japan are a feast for the eyes. They can be enjoyed by both passers-by and the happy few who can actually afford to shop in such places. Window displays mirror our increasingly materialistic world in much the same way as advertisements do. And like ads, the presentations that line our streets are an important point of contact with potential customers. Considerable creativity is put into publicizing seasonal collections, especially at the top end of the retail market. Luxury retailers, in particular, have raised the window display to something of an art form. They give as much attention to their street presence as to any other vehicle of publicity.

Hermès Japan understands that the shop window is more than a platform for showcasing the latest bag or belt. The window forms an interface between fashion house and public. It communicates what the brand represents. Leila Menchari has been the sole creator of window displays at the Hermès store in Paris since 1977. But at Maison Hermès, the big Hermès outlet in Ginza, Tokyo, the retailer has worked with no fewer than ten international artists and designers on a series of rotating displays since the store opened in 2001. Designed by Renzo Piano, Maison Hermès is a serene ten-storey edifice wrapped almost entirely in blank façades of glass block. Inside, retail floors are topped by offices and, on the uppermost level, a small cinema. Though the store's two window displays are dwarfed beneath the huge expanse of glazing, they do overlook Ginza's main commercial thoroughfare, with its steady stream of shoppers, office workers and tourists passing by.

Exploiting this location to the full, Hermès has developed a coherent concept for window arrangements based on simple narratives that are easy to read yet always visually clever. A minuscule theatre, the Hermès win-

Continued on page 136

Through th Loc

Text by SHONQUIS MORENO
Photography by
DAVID HLYNSKY

A pane of glass, not more than 1.5 centimetres thick, divides the shop from the pavement. On one side, the climate-controlled interior welcomes those who can buy; on the other, the intemperate street is where those who cannot buy may look without paying in the time-honoured ritual of window-shopping. Glass is technically a solid

cheer up and to shop to affirm t we are fashionab our parents, tha gress.

While windo store's marketi scends those go us. They expres nature, catalogu make us laugh they are epher seasons, record itics, our charac times. If they

king Glass

ss ourselves. We
ve are free, that
at we are *not* like
are making pro-

sign forwards a
als, it also tran-
Windows describe
ideals, evoke our
r aspirations and
three. Although
, they mark the
ment in our pol-
ur fantasies, our
ted, boxed care-

vaudevillians, doodlers, admen, curators, stylists, sideshow barkers, carpenters, craftsmen, graphic designers,
OCD sufferers and cultural weathervanes. It was with the widening advent of plate glass in the 1890s that
the shop window began its journey towards a new millennium. At first, windows comprised abundant piles of
merchandise to indicate what was in
stock. In 1894 wax mannequins replaced dressmaker's forms at the Paris
Exposition. Around the dawn of the
twentieth century, *The Show Window*
magazine (founded by the author of

Window-dressers are scenarists, vaudevillians, doodlers, admen, curators, stylists, sideshow barkers, carpenters, craftsmen, graphic designers, OCD sufferers and cultural weathervanes. Their windows forward a store's marketing goals, but also describe us

INTRODUCTION

— Russian military fashion: shirts and epaulettes (1990).

Through the Looking Glass

**Text by SHONQUIS MORENO
Photography by
DAVID HLYNSKY**

A pane of glass, not more than 1.5 centimetres thick, divides the shop from the pavement. On one side, the climate-controlled interior welcomes those who can buy; on the other, the intemperate street is where those who cannot buy may look without paying in the time-honoured ritual of window-shopping. Glass is technically a solid liquid, a magical paradox linking the 'real' world with a world of luxury. At their finest, the displays behind it are magical, too – greater by far than the sum of their parts.

Enclosed-window retail display, the high-end kind in which a temporary *mise en scène* revolves around expensive merchandise, has been neglected as a design discipline, yet it continues to play a role in the broader culture. Windows tell stories about us and the desires that drive us. Consider Truman Capote's *Breakfast at Tiffany's*, in which patrician displays of jewellery are the object of Holly Golightly's yearning to transform herself from the provincial Lula Mae Barnes into the cosmopolitan wife of a diplomat, kept safely behind glass. Street-level retail windows are largely removed from the vicissitudes of the street (if not from its fashions), their purpose being to create experiences – usually flights, or cheeky dips, of fancy – that generate sales, communicate a brand and cultivate a particular clientele.

In the West, consumption is a cultural imperative and a duty, and globalization is exporting this rite to the rest of the world. Shopping draws the citizen of democracy into the fold just as *not* shopping casts him out. It assigns us a station in the social order. By shopping, we explore who we are and where we belong; what we buy identifies us to others. We shop compulsively – to relax, to kill time, to procrastinate, to keep up with the Joneses. We shop to release tension, to cheer up and to express ourselves. We shop to affirm that we are free, that we are fashionable, that we are *not* like our parents, that we are making progress.

While window design forwards a store's marketing goals, it also transcends those goals. Windows describe us. They express our ideals, evoke our nature, catalogue our aspirations and make us laugh at all three. Although they are ephemeral, they mark the seasons, record a moment in our politics, our characters, our fantasies, our times. If they persisted, boxed carefully away, they would provide rich artefacts for future archaeologists. Best of all, they cost the passer-by nothing. They are relatively democratic; the Française who escapes the suburban shopping mall in St-Denis for an afternoon on the Champs Elysees may look as long as she likes. Yet what display windows point at, and

---

*Windows describe us.
They express our ideals, evoke
our nature, catalogue our
aspirations and make us
laugh at all three*

---

push us towards, is financially inaccessible to many people much of the time. In one way, this is the pitfall and the virtue of a free market. Windows epitomize privilege: with the exception of jewellery display, the bigger and thicker the glazing, the bigger the privilege. This is demonstrated by windows on Rodeo Drive in Los Angeles as bluntly as it is laid out in Amsterdam's red-light district, where the dimensions of the display is in direct proportion to the cost of the merchandise. The fact that display appeals to our ambitions is part of why it appeals to our imaginations. Even if you were to buy each piece of merchandise in the window, would you be able to re-create the dream?

Window-dressers are scenarists, vaudevillians, doodlers, admen, curators, stylists, sideshow barkers, carpenters, craftsmen, graphic designers, OCD sufferers and cultural weathervanes. It was with the widening advent of plate glass in the 1890s that the shop window began its journey towards a new millennium. At first, windows comprised abundant piles of merchandise to indicate what was in stock. In 1894 wax mannequins replaced dressmaker's forms at the Paris Exposition. Around the dawn of the twentieth century, *The Show Window* magazine (founded by the author of *The Wizard of Oz* books) encouraged retailers to be more thoughtful in the selection and presentation of objects and to exploit the new electric light. Shop windows became a tool in the education of modern designers. Today, dressers work with more wide-ranging materials than almost any artist or craftsman in order to create narratives, swatches of narratives, images or impressions. They work with candy, ladies' wigs, housing insulation, packets of synthetic sweetener, live ducks, female art students, a kilometre of phone cord, carefully composed light and shadow, even slices of grilled bread. They walk a fine line between cultivating exclusivity and letting the rest of us down so softly that we feel uplifted. For decades, the role of window-dresser has been played by guest artists, struggling artists, stylists, photographers, curators and the editors of glossy magazines. The unsung casts of window-display freelancers are often pulled from the ranks of art school graduates and remain largely anonymous, hidden in plain sight, working before and after hours to perfect studied tableaux by being exceptionally resourceful. Although the community of window-dressers includes people as celebrated as artists Salvador Dali, Andy Warhol, Robert Rauschenberg and Jasper Johns, as well as industrial designers Donald Deskey and Henry Dreyfuss, window design has been, and continues to be, a (refined and generous) form of advertising.

— Moscow, Russia (1990). Jewellery shop display.

Few countries in the world, however, support significant numbers of window-dressers. The species tends to flourish only in major urban centres populated with lavish retail establishments. In the United States, Western Europe and Japan, for instance, display tends to prosper. (In America, there are more than 5.5 billion square feet of retail space to fill.) Loping towards a free market and tight-reined democracy, Russia – a nation that should be developing display muscles – garners global attention not for street-level scenarios behind glass, but for the six people a day who fall, jump or are pushed out of windows far above the streets of Moscow. A number of Eastern European countries have relatively few shops to support Gucci-quality display. Photographer David Hlynsky documented the retail windows of Communist Europe (Russia, Bulgaria, Yugoslavia) during the late 1980s. His images record windows filled with essential, banal items – bread, meat, cheese, simple clothing – a sharp contrast to the decadent windows of the West. 'To not shop,' writes Hlynsky, 'is to not pay attention.' Architect Rem Koolhaas has taken this idea a step further in his latest interiors for couturier Miuccia Prada, as well as in recent publications. Koolhaas believes the city has fallen

Window-dressers walk a fine line between cultivating exclusivity and letting the rest of us down so softly that we feel uplifted

wholly under the influence of shopping. Museums, cathedrals, theatres, football stadiums – all contain space dedicated to buying things. To not participate in consumption is to not participate in contemporary culture.

In one sense, rules of display at Chanel Paris are the same as those at de Bijenkorf in the Netherlands, which are the same as those at Wal-Mart in Baton Rouge, Louisiana: The window must capture the eye of the pedestrian in an instant. At Wal-Mart, however, the goal is to create desire indiscriminately. The firm does not try to generate a flight of the imagination, but to induce what many English-speaking parents have long called 'the gimmes': the desire to possess everything in sight. Sometimes these types of windows are so familiar to us that we either cease to register them fully or we begin to use them as a compass in unfamiliar territory. One McDonald's restaurant resembles all the rest, in terms of both design and menu. The same applies to the Gap and Banana Republic, with their globally syndicated, cookie-cutter displays. The phenomenon is endemic to mass consumption, as opposed to the more precious acquisition that occurs at upscale shops.

At the retail level of companies like Prada, Hermès and Bergdorf Goodman, window-dressers have a relatively broad range of expression. At Barneys New York, Simon Doonan caricatures international celebrities, praising and parodying them simultaneously. He makes a subtle comment about safe sex by putting a couple of gold-wrapped condoms in a window with the sculpture of an HIV-positive celeb, or a more pointed visual comment about the politics of a notoriously bigoted politician. Sometimes this commentary strikes a chord with the public, engendering complaints and media coverage; considering American prudery, however, free speech is surprisingly at liberty in Doonan's windows. Artist Barbara Kruger's 2004 Boxing Day display for London department store Selfridges blatantly disparaged consumerism with slogans like 'Buyer Beware' and 'We are slaves to the objects around us'. If we're cynical, the installation comes off as a hypocritical gimmick, exploiting 'art' that purports to be a critique of consumerism in order to fuel consumerism itself. The Selfridges marketing director envisioned Kruger's

windows as a tool to depict the store as up to date, and was comfortable using irony to speak to its clientele – a clientele that he thought would embrace the message as an affirmation of its own beliefs. Are we fooling ourselves? It is an attitude that may be as much of an indulgence and compulsion as shopping: We are aware of our

Loping towards a free market and tight-reined democracy, Russia – a nation that should be developing display muscles – garners global attention not for street-level scenarios behind glass, but for the six people a day who fall, jump or are pushed out of windows far above the streets of Moscow

addiction, of course, and we could quit (consuming) any time we really wanted to.

The very notion of manufacturing desire is perilous – we like to crave things out of reach and then resent the unsatisfied longing. Many people who enjoy this brand of 'street theatre' can't afford the merchandise: We look rather than buy, and those with buying power, rushing between a dark-windowed limo and a private fitting room, hardly look at all. An extreme example is Jeffrey's in Atlanta and New York, whose owner has been known to ship clothes to clients for at-home fitting and selection; like the Queen, they never have to travel to the store at all.

The pull exerted by things desired exudes a paradoxical quality, contained in display windows (and in us), the window sometimes becomes the object on which we act out various passions. During the midsummer 1977 blackout in New York City, simmer-

— Moscow, Russia (1990). Subway map of central Moscow, displayed at a large toy store.

— Crakow, Poland (1988): Three loaves of bread.

most
es a
mes
mes
lows
mit-
re-
rish-
like,
can
f, at
e of

— Crakow, Poland (1989). Nightdresses and knickers behind a butterfly print.

ing racial and class prejudices (and a severe heat wave) boiled over into the streets when the lights went out for 25 hours across four of the city's five boroughs. People in some of the more impoverished neighbourhoods (unemployment among young African-Americans stood at a Depression-level 40 per cent in some areas) shattered display windows to loot Pontiacs, colour TVs, sneakers, even sink stoppers and clothes pegs. Hospital emergency rooms were crowded with the injured, many of whom were admitted with lacerations caused by plate glass.

Luxury exerts a certain intimidating aloofness – which may account for the fact that not a single window on posh Fifth Avenue was broken during the 1977 looting – but it is also vulnerable to our collective moods. On two nights known as *Kristallnacht* in November 1939, broken windows signified the single most brutal economic and physical blow to the Jewish population of Germany and Austria up to that point. Almost 7500 Jewish businesses were destroyed and six million marks paid out by insurance companies to replace windows. Germany had to import plate glass from Belgium to repair all the damage. Conversely, we are vulnerable to the 'mood' of windows. To many, broken windows (like graffiti) signify decay, a lack of attention, a loss of control – a Hobbesian condition. Whole windows embody order, the rule of law and a guarantee of personal safety. Whole shop windows, even more than others, point to

Whole shop windows, even more than others, point to a degree of order and well-being that is comforting, uplifting and frustrating, simultaneously

a degree of order and wellbeing that is comforting, uplifting and frustrating, simultaneously.

In recent years, display budgets have been increasingly folded into marketing budgets. Old-school window-dressing is being replaced by direct-mail campaigns, syndicated Gap-style windows, complex interior displays and commercial websites. Sales-orientated

— Ja
Java
of ab

— Hand coloured portraits. Skopje, Macedonia, Yugoslavia, 1989.

websites, or virtual product presentations, are the latest incarnation of display windows. They can't be shattered, they won't be shuttered and they can be accessed from almost any computer in the world, day or night. Founded in 1995, eBay is no less than 'the world's online marketplace' and hosts tens of millions of members from all over the globe. Though ugly to look at, it is functional, and surfers spend more time on eBay than on any other website. It cannot be doubted that the quality of the design of this type of 'window' will become ever more significant to the online business model.

By now, many stores and shopping malls have eliminated enclosed windows completely. The days when people used to stand on the pavement and marvel at displays are not gone, but they are somewhat faded. We are no longer expected to ogle fripperies in glass cases; we're expected to walk up and grab what we want. It's likely that glass-enclosed displays will become more meaningful to us as they become

> **Sales-orientated websites, or virtual product presentations, are the latest incarnation of display windows**

rarer. Scarcity seems to be what most powerfully elevates and preserves a craft today: as its practice becomes more and more impractical, it assumes an increasingly artistic aura. Windows continue to serve as brilliant, if limited, tools for advertising. The fact remains that excellent design is nourishing to maker and viewer alike, whether or not window-shoppers can buy what is being marketed. If, at times, windows seem to be the face of an arch let-them-eat-cake elitism, they are also a fertile, protected realm in which any mind can stretch itself. It's what each person chooses to take away from the windows that is significant: Looking without buying may make us richer in more ways than one.

— Jakarta, Indonesia (8 January 1999). Indonesian rioters looting a shoe shop in Karawang, West Java, scale the walls of the building. Two men are killed when police open fire on a rampaging mob of about 2000, a crowd that later indulges in an orgy of looting and arson.

The Th

seco

By SHONQUIS MORENO
Photography by
RICKY ZEHAVI
& JOHN CORDES

ree-
nd Rule

and tourists, while 57th Street has a view of the cross-town bus and 58th Street supports residential traffic and grannies with cotton-candy hair and crocodile handbags, guests of the

Window displays at Bergdorf Goodman do more than entice passers-by into this venerable New York department store. They sustain a tradition by blending advertising and street theatre into a very public form of installation art, understandable at a glance

BERGDORF GOODMAN

The Three-second Rule

By SHONQUIS MORENO
Photography by
RICKY ZEHAVI
& JOHN CORDES

NEW YORK — Entrances to Bergdorf Goodman's display windows are through a series of secret doors hidden in the rococo walls of the store's interior. The Fifth Avenue windows, for instance, open into the jewellery department. Being inside the windows, installing displays, combines exposure to and protection from the street. The Fifth Avenue windows look out at a pageant of fashionistas and tourists, while 57th Street has a view of the cross-town bus and 58th Street supports residential traffic and grannies with cotton-candy hair and crocodile handbags, guests of the Plaza Hotel. It is in a cluttered workshop on Bergdorf's eighth floor that the store's window displays are conceived. At various times a visitor might find the labyrinthine rooms of the Visual Department crammed with strips of Mylar, pink housing insulation, mattresses and metal flashing, curling reams of wood veneer and bendy board. A series of cubbyholes stuffed with mannequins reveals standing, twisting, reclining, surprised and abstract figures. There are naked tree branches and man-made objects – hangers, dress forms, chair frames – so worn they evoke the character of natural materials like driftwood or seaglass. A couple of miles away in Queens, an entire warehouse provides storage for Bergdorf's remaining display props.

Display design is a field that synthesizes skills of all kinds – some almost obsolete in the world beyond the glass – yet is neglected as a design dis-

'We're drawn to extremes here. We like minimalism and we like maximalism. We're not so crazy about medium-ism.'
David Hoey

cipline. Bergdorf's windows are a reminder of this discrepancy. Last year's Cooper-Hewitt National Design Museum Triennial included a window created by Bergdorf's window director,

— Looking into the windows of Bergdorf Goodman is like looking into a person's face. The Fifth Avenue display windows are designed to attract the attention of all within viewing distance: motorists rushing by or stuck in traffic, shoppers in a hurry, the daily lunch-hour crowd, and tourists with time and money to spare.

MARC JACOBS
04 TRUNK SHOW
WEDNESDAY, MAY 12 – FRIDAY, MAY 14
11:00 – 6:00
ON 3

— Two ostriches crafted of torn paper were part of the Bergdorf summer 2004 menagerie. 'We had to hire people,' says Hoey, 'just to sit around and tear paper for about two weeks.'

YVES SAINT LAUR
RIVE GAUCHE
OUR EXPANDED BOUTIQUE

— Hoey's team filled several summer 2003 windows with uncrowned bodies, emphasizing the graphic nature of human geometry. Clustered in the background, a variety of busts, made of diverse materials and representing different time periods, gaze into space. The mannequin in the foreground wears a creation by Yves Saint Laurent.

— Window dressers develop an eye that turns everything they see into potential display props. For a series of Narciso Rodriguez windows from autumn 2000, three of Hoey's staff spent a week grilling hundreds of slices of bread to create a wall covering.

GUCCI
THE NEW BOUTIQUE

— This page and next page: emphasizing the graphic nature of the human form, Hoey's team filled several summer 2003 windows with disembodied legs and hands.

YVES SAINT LAUR[ENT]
RIVE GAUCHE
OUR EXPANDED BOUTIQUE

— Hoey's team filled several summer 2003 windows with uncrowned bodies, emphasizing the graphic nature of human geometry. Clustered in the background, a variety of busts, made of diverse materials and representing different time periods, gaze into space. The mannequin in the foreground wears a creation by Yves Saint Laurent.

SATISFY YOUR SHOE CRAVING
BERGDORF GOODMAN'S NEW SHOE SALON ON 2
OPEN AUGUST 3

— In celebration of the opening of Bergdorf's new shoe department in June 2002, Hoey papered the rear wall of the window with a blow-up of the actual blueprint of the new space. The overhead perspective is a Bergdorf signature.

— Hoey calls the scene in this autumn 2003 window, dedicated to all things Manolo Blahnik, 'insanely maxed-out'. 'We're crazy,' he says. 'You couldn't put a speck more in that window.'

— 'Bergdorf blondes are a *thing*, you know, a New York craze. Absolutely everyone wants to be one…' The quote on the display window is from *Bergdorf Blondes*, a novel by Plum Sykes. Hoey's collection of wigs, brushes, combs and hair accessories gave an imaginative twist to the publication of the book, an event that ushered in the spring of 2004 and planted a pressing question in many a New Yorker's mind: How can *I* become a Bergdorf blonde?

They sustain a tradition by blending advertising and street theatre into a very public form of installation art, understandable at a glance

SHOP WINDOW DESIGN

BERGDORF GOODMAN

– David Hoey. In an effort to solve a recurring problem – how to display 30 handbags at once – Hoey placed a mannequin at one side of a window and extended her arm, à la Salvador Dalí, 4.88 metres to the far wall, hanging a profusion of bags, like bracelets, down the length of her prolific limb.

Hoey's windows, in particular, are uniquely graphic, textural, humorous and avant-garde. In a window cele-

'Window designers develop an eye that turns anything you look at into a potential prop – from a ton of dyed turkey feathers to a kilometre of telephone wire.'
David Hoey

brating *Visionaire* magazine, Hoey again played with surrealism and distortion. By sheathing the window in a box, he created a forced perspective. Inside, a mannequin's legs telescoped impossibly upwards, Alice in Wonderland-style, so that her head disappeared through a trapdoor in the ceiling and reappeared beside her feet on the floor below. Hoey's is an arch humour, camp and tongue-in-cheek.

— In search of a fresh way to display dozens of handbags in a single window, Hoey found a solution in summer 2002 that would have suited Salvador Dalí to a T.

He'll pair a quarter-million-dollar Venetian cut-glass mirror with 1970s mirrored light bulbs. 'We're drawn to extremes here. We like minimalism, and we like maximalism. We're not so crazy about medium-ism,' says Hoey. 'We want our minimal windows to be maximal in effect, through an economy of means.'

In a series of Hoey's windows dedicated to music, a toy piano cast the looming shadow of a grand piano against the rear wall, while the shadow of a mannequin was shaped like a piano bench instead of a woman. He also loves to distort scale. Using vastly exaggerated construction blueprints for another project, he 'carpeted' the rear wall, on which two mannequins were seated perpendicular to the glass, thus creating a scene that read as an overhead perspective. Instead of building out the props of the room around the mannequins, he forced the viewer to use the blueprint symbols to fill in visual details – a door here, a window there.

'A future anthropologist could learn a lot from analyzing what went into New York's display windows: what was happening in international design, fashion, high culture, popular culture.'
David Hoey

Not surprisingly, Hoey lists Lewis Carroll, Alfred Hitchcock and Rube Goldberg among his influences. He delights in themes and variations on themes, riffing on a single idea to make multiple windows form a series on a single subject or work together as a diptych or triptych. He likes to show action frozen in time or to transform sound into something visual. The design is synaesthetic, criss-crossing between both graphic and tactile. Hoey and his team have built walls from white gift boxes and pillowy pink rectangles of housing insulation. They have crafted '70s-style wall hangings out of hundreds of women's wigs. One window required three staff members to spend a week grilling countless slices of bread for a sculpture of toast.

Fall Handbag Picks on

— Hoey uses materials, such as housing insulation (1999), that are both graphic and tactile. Numbering Lewis Carroll and Rube Goldberg among his influences, Hoey treated a mannequin's legs like taffy in a February 2003 window: Disappearing through a trapdoor in the ceiling, her head reappears through the floor beside her feet.

DONNA KARAN
ON 3

— In autumn 2002, hand-cut black felt crafted by a fleet of extraordinary freelancers evoked a storm in a Donna Karan display.

— In a literal interpretation of the display term 'flying merchandise' (which refers to the suspension of objects from monofilament or fishing line), Hoey flies a mannequin and all her accessories in the summer of 2004.

Another display, featuring stretchy latex pulled across a cello, showed the bare outlines of the instrument pushing against the fabric and into the window. (Music is nothing if not felt.) Bergdorf windows tend to make the familiar unfamiliar, and vice versa.

Having studied music, art and design, Hoey worked in music before coming to windows at Neiman Marcus in Dallas. After moving to Manhattan in 1994, he became a freelance producer of events, displays and fashion shows. 'I knew I wanted to do windows when I saw a photograph of a 1949 Bonwit Teller window that showed an impeccably dressed mannequin with

two heads,' says Hoey. 'Gene Moore, the 20th century's greatest window dresser, wanted to show a woman who loved hats so much that she grew an extra head.' New York City is one of the few places in the United States imbued with a human-scale, street-level, shoulder-to-shoulder experience of place. During the late 1930s, New York windows entered a golden era in which surrealist display came into vogue. Briefly in the '70s, windows by Candy Pratts at Bloomingdale's, Robert Courrier at Henri Bendel and Victor Hugo at Halston Street Level were filled with street theater – moody tableaux with dark narratives, murky

symbolism and controversial, quasi-sadomasochistic scenes.

In 1997 Hoey joined Linda Fargo, Vice President of Visual Merchandising at Bergdorf. Fargo, whose book *Dreams Through the Glass* (Assouline, 2003) brings together her recent display work, is renowned for her exquisite, thickly detailed Christmas windows. In contrast, Hoey is at his finest when taking a more Spartan approach. 'My windows have a baroque romanticism,' says Fargo. 'David's have a shocking, humorous, graphic sensibility that's very inventive.' (In parallel with their design styles, Fargo describes her apartment

JILL STUART
ON 5IVE

as a 'closet' cluttered with objects, while Hoey calls his 'an empty container'.) Through Hoey's windows, Bergdorf looks back, stylistically, to mid-century display, updated to express today's ideas and to anticipate tomorrow's.

Bergdorf has the tallest windows in the city, and Hoey's team is responsible for filling 35 of them on a regular basis. Some are jewellery-display-size 'shadowbox' windows, and others are glazed spaces as large as 3.96 metres high and 6.10 metres long. Variations on a single design concept can mean that up to 400 discrete ideas go up yearly.

The word 'we' is used a lot around the offices and for good reason. 'My Rolodex is the first thing I'd grab in a fire,' says Hoey who calls on a stable of freelancers – painters, a neon artist, sound producers, sculptors in various media, graphic designers, illustrators and stylists – many of whom have been trained as fine artists. Versatile and resourceful, they write on walls, for example, with everything from candle smoke to chocolate bars. Work inside the windows involves handling tools, scraping walls, painting out windows in preparation for the next display and, for example, hot-gluing thousands of leaves to a wall. Touch-up

staff work late at night or early in the morning, before the store opens, squeezing into tight spots to add a dot of white paint to a scratched floor, to tuck in wires, straighten frames. Others, like Johanna Burke, who studied photography and installation art and has been freelancing at Bergdorf for seven years, fabricate custom pieces. 'David starts with a free-floating idea and makes a series of scribbles decipherable only to a handful of trained individuals,' says Burke. 'He talks through the idea with the people in the studio and then, when installation begins, he wings it.' Tight deadlines force the team to use thumbnail

— 'Ridiculous carnival confections,' says Hoey of a series of five windows from spring 2004 that were filled with prizewinning cakes, candyfloss, snow cones, popcorn and saltwater taffy. The candyfloss coifs, fur and wallpaper in this window were created by spray-painting cotton upholstery batting.

— Hoey and his team dip into a diversity of materials, including the pink housing insulation used for these pillows (1999), to create scenes both graphic and tactile.

— Q is for 'quaint', a word unrelated to Bergdorf's 2003 holiday windows. Hoey lined the 57th Street displays with an alphabet of objects, A to Z, found or made by his extraordinary stable of freelance artists. Of the staff members who

sketches and verbal shorthand rather than formal drawings. The five-person, full-time staff keep 'idea drawers' containing scraps of paper, illustrations, favourite paint chips and pages torn from catalogues. Installation takes place on site with a self-imposed 18-hour deadline, similar in intensity to an architectural *charrette*. Shifts last as long as it takes, and most freelancers can count on 12-hour days, at least. Pedestrians who stop to chat

offer well-worn advice like 'A little to the left' or 'That picture's crooked'.

Hoey believes in the three E's of window display – Entice, Educate and Entertain – and in 'the three-second rule'. Like a billboard, the window should make its point at a single glance. Bergdorf's windows, however, also bear up under scrutiny. They are never explicit. They can be an intellectual puzzle, a tiny report on the state of popular culture. 'David's win-

dows work on three scales of motion, which all windows must but which his do extra well,' says curator Donald Albrecht, who chose Hoey's windows for the Cooper-Hewitt Triennial. 'The motorist gets a great visual impression and the pedestrian who doesn't stop gets the same. Then, for those who have the time to actually stop and look, there's still lots to see that the others miss.'

'Looking into the windows is like

made the larger-than-life, wood-veneer horse and paper-bellows camera, Hoey says: 'I have geniuses on the staff.'

looking into someone's face,' says Fargo. If the store is the flesh, the windows are evidence of its spirit, and Bergdorf is a person we'd all like to know, or be. Hoey uses, and is often inspired by, collections borrowed from individuals: antique dress forms, phones, vacuum cleaners, sewing machines, hangers. 'Sometimes clothes are the inspiration. That should be the case 100 per cent of the time, but it doesn't always work that way,' says

Hoey. On special occasions, windows promote book and magazine launches, museum exhibitions or auction-house sales. 'Window designers develop an eye that turns anything you look at into a potential prop,' says Hoey. 'We've tried to exploit the artistic capabilities of everything from a ton of dyed turkey feathers to a kilometre of telephone wire. We love doing big tangles and jumbles of ordinary objects. I've even calculated how many

Post-It notes it would take to cover a wall.'

Hoey describes display as equal parts theatre, advertising, installation art, fashion and storytelling. 'Our windows tell all,' says Hoey. 'A future anthropologist could learn a lot from analyzing what went into New York's display windows: what was happening in international design, fashion, high culture, pop culture, you name it.' So can we.

CISO RODRIGUEZ
ON 3

— An immense blonde hairdo graces the rear walls of a spring 2004 window, proclaiming the launch of the novel entitled *Bergdorf Blondes*.

sketd
than
perse
draw
illust
page
latio
impc
inter
Shift
freela
at lea

Reuters/WFA

London, UK (1 May 2000). A protester smashes the window of a money-exchange office during May-Day disturbances in Central London. Sporadic violence marred the capital's May-Day marches as demonstrators ransacked a McDonald's restaurant and threw bottles at Prime Minister Tony Blair's official residence.

On a M

By SARAH MARTÍN PEARSON
Photography by
LLUÍS CAPDEVILA MARTÍN

BARCELONA — A landmark in
Barcelona's design culture, Vinçon is

ission

joining building, La Pedrera, a work by Antonio Gaudí.

Vinçon's focus is on design as a vehicle of communication with a conceptual basis, a creative discipline that invigorates the mind and, in so doing, lifts design to a cultural level. In short, good design has a positive influence on

Window displays at Vinçon, a Barcelona shop specializing in designer products, are not strictly commercial; they reflect the owners' vision of what good design is all about: functionality, aesthetics and affordability

VINÇON

On a Mission

— This 1940s window display features crockery and a variety of other household items. Photography by Vinçon.

By SARAH MARTÍN PEARSON
Photography by
LLUÍS CAPDEVILA MARTÍN

BARCELONA — A landmark in Barcelona's design culture, Vinçon is backed by a long tradition in the sale of contemporary household appliances. Infused by a sense of innovation, this family-run business is well rooted in a philosophy that draws strength from design. Only a year after Hugo Vinçon founded the company in 1934, the Amat family entered the scene; today, seven decades later, they are still at the helm. Vinçon could not have a better location: Passeig de Gràcia is a central area of the city enriched by modernist architecture. The building Vinçon occupies was once the home of Ramon Casas (1845-1899), a Catalan painter known for his gypsy themes and advertising illustrations. The first floor, currently the furniture department, enjoys direct access to one of the city's more beautiful inner courtyards with a direct view of an ad-

joining building, La Pedrera, a work by Antonio Gaudí.

Vinçon's focus is on design as a vehicle of communication with a conceptual basis, a creative discipline that invigorates the mind and, in so doing, lifts design to a cultural level. In short, good design has a positive influence on society. This explains why, since 1973, the former artist's studio accommo-

Antonio Iglesias's training as a dancer surfaces in the choreographic dynamic of window displays in which objects appear frozen in time

dates Sala Vinçon, a multipurpose space in which art exhibitions and product presentations promote the cultural aspects of design-based disciplines. Similarly, Vinçon's window displays often bypass the strictly commercial in an attempt to convey a

philosophical concept of design.

Third-generation manager Sergio Amat emphasizes this cultural approach. 'Our commercial principle is to choose objects that offer a perfectly balanced fusion of functionality, ergonomics, price and aesthetics,' he says. 'We don't want to sell an oil dispenser that drips, a chair that's uncomfortable or any other object that doesn't fulfil its purpose.' Vinçon's window displays reflect his view that 'functionality is key', together with good-looking, affordably priced merchandise.

Over the years, a number of top window-dressers have created these

— A photograph from the 1940s shows Vinçon's original façade and shop entrance, with lettering indicating the owner's name. Photography by Vinçon.

displays, always influenced by the ideas of proprietors Fernando and Sergio Amat. Currently responsible for a task previously carried out by skilful predecessors such as Antoni Casas, Jordi Nogués and Ramon Pujol is Antonio Iglesias. Formerly a dancer, stage producer, choreographer and costume designer, Iglesias found a vocation in window-dressing after teaming up with window-whiz Pujol as a part-time assistant 12 years ago. The

'I prefer to work directly on the scene, to experiment with the composition and the effect created by different materials until, suddenly, something clicks.' Antonio Iglesias

work evolved into a full-time job. At a certain point he abandoned his theatrical pursuits for the opportunity to replace his tutor. Iglesias's training as a dancer surfaces in the choreographic dynamic of displays in which objects appear frozen in time. And the theatrical aspect of his personality emerges in crowd-drawing windows that feature live performers doing a model's hair or teaching onlookers how to prepare a Spanish omelette.

Antonio Iglesias recalls Pujol's windows as carefully staged scenarios based on meticulous plans and preliminary sketches. Motivated by a more intuitive approach, Iglesias 'prefers to work directly on the scene'. He likes to 'experiment with the composition and the effects created by different materials until, suddenly, something clicks'.

'We talk about our ideas before taking action,' says Sergio Amat. 'Later on, Antonio finds a way to express them while working in the window itself.' Many of their ideas involve the promotion of new products. 'Otherwise,' says Amat, 'we like to change our windows about every three weeks.' Three-week intervals have proved successful in holding the public's attention and in attracting return customers. Iglesias agrees with Amat, who says that 'a shop window marks a start and an end' and should appeal to people to come back for more. Together they have used windows to create customer loyalty among visitors who look forward to the latest display of what's new on the 'design scene'.

— A collection of handcrafted rope furniture, suitable for both indoor and outdoor use, carries a tropical theme. Reinforcing the Caribbean atmosphere are a turquoise wall and a scattering of bananas. Simple, yet effective.

Amat believes a crucial part of their success is the small but select company of qualified window-dressers that preceded Iglesias, whose work he is also quick to praise. 'All our window-dressers earned Vinçon's confidence by learning the company philosophy inside out,' he says. Past efforts led to displays that projected clear ideas, and Iglesias's designs are no exception. Windows often feature household articles in a surprising setting, scenes that hint of a humorous backstory, a narrative that brings inanimate objects to life and gives them personality. Repetition is a favourite device, as is a focus on an object's functional qualities. Using the window frame as a container for big piles of the article being highlighted is another of Iglesias's practices. He is also known for creating unusual, sometimes surreal, domestic scenes to display furniture. Symbolism is a regular result of his imaginative concepts. A prime example is the window that presented a black leather sofa draped with a spotlit cape, a scene carefully put together to evoke images of a snorting bull pawing the dirt in the *plaza de toros*.

Collaborating with colleagues in the retail business can also lead to intriguing windows. Good relations between the Amats and the owners of Camper shoes, for example, have led to displays featuring footwear and, on one occasion, the declaration 'Vinçon loves Camper'. Another window revolved

— Marking the end of the year, the pages of a calendar strewn across this display appear to have escaped from large envelopes attached to the wall; the window also ushers in the new year with a custom-designed calendar created for Vinçon by graphic artist América Sánchez.

— To promote an art exhibition held at Sala Vinçon, the store put the work of Colombian pop artist Gabriel Ortega in the window. Ortega's distinctive black-and-white paintings are set against a backdrop of bold stripes. A row of plastic 'zebras' made in Africa lines the bottom of the window, adding a hint of humour to the display.

— When the Prestige oil spills brought environmental tragedy to Galicia in 2002, window-dresser Antonio Iglesias expressed his solidarity with the victims through this display. Images of volunteers in white jump suits and Wellington boots lugging buckets of the thick tar that covered the coast were worldwide news. Iglesias used an aluminium dustbin for sale in the store, but the wellies were his. The artificial seagull became so popular that, when Vinçon decided to stock the item, the shop was quickly sold out.

— A squatter-inspired scene provides the rough look needed for Martí Guixé's T-shirt collection for Cha-Chá, a series of shirts devoted to such contemporary Barcelona celebrities as Chef, Ex-designer, Consumer, Social Artist and DJ. Featured is a row of dilapidated upholstered seating partially draped with T-shirts. Glass deliberately marred by scratches and dirt makes viewing the display a bit of a challenge.

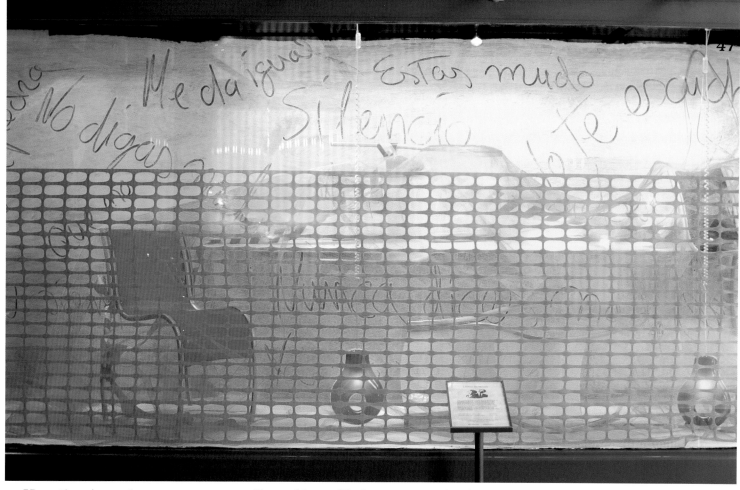

— Here the viewer happens upon a traffic accident. Chairs appear to be the victims of a crash, orange plastic fencing marks off the danger zone, and scrawled across the rear wall are the alarmed comments of passers-by: I'm speechless… Can't hear anything… Don't tell me… What a racket!… On display are Kartell chairs in transparent red Plexiglas and Metalarte's Lifelight lamp. The expanse of orange mesh pays homage to Cristo, the artist renowned for wrapping gigantic structures in fabric.

— Top Secret lamps by Metalarte add to the cluttered look of the window (seen here from the side) featuring Zanotta's black leather sofa.

— A collection of 'tapas bar' articles by Cha-Chá – each labelled 'Casa Lolo' – called for an appropriate display. The window includes typical tapas-bar elements, such as a blackboard for the menu, an apron and some cute 'seafood snacks', all of which form an inviting context for the colourfully packaged items in Cha-Chá's collection.

— A display announcing the arrival of a new collection of Japanese products presents a mishmash of Oriental items, from chopsticks and soup plates to place mats and sake sets, an organized muddle filled with a sense of animation.

— A typically urban setting showcases the quality of Zanotta's black leather sofa, here seen in a simulated metro station peppered with the flyaway pages of a newspaper. Lights, along with white stripes on the rear wall, evoke the idea of a tube train speeding by.

— A display protesting the war in Iraq features the workspace of George W. Bush (as imagined by Iglesias), an area of absolute chaos: crumpled papers scattered across the floor, splinters of wood, ballpoints and pencils pinned at random to the wall, and a flurry of catastrophe-related terms penned in a large hand (hurricane, cyclone, tornado and the like).

— Adjacent to the window displaying scattered calendar pages is a 'window in white' presenting Kartell's Plexiglas chairs. Here water bottles from the chair display merge into the neighbouring window, providing an element of interplay between the two scenes.

— Sala Vinçon hosted an exhibition (Minimalanimal) devoted to a group of Portuguese designers and their Zen-inspired ceramics, a group of objects with an organic look borrowed from nature. Some of the exhibition pieces appearing in this window display were later sold in the store.

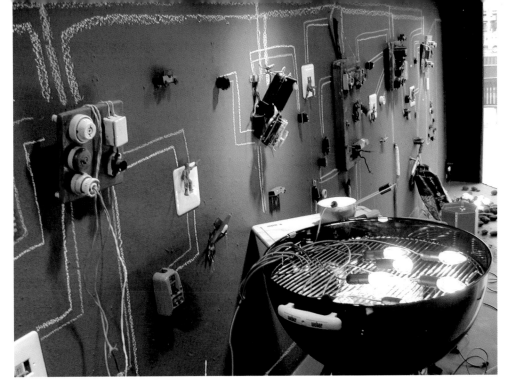

— A protest of the war in Iraq moves from Bush to the battlefield. A barbecue grill full of light bulbs and a rough sketch of an old-fashioned electrical circuit board wrap the scene in a cloak of unease. An arsenal of rubber tanks, boats and soldiers are simulated in the layout of a supposed battle. Dark paint conjures up the perfect blackboard effect for unveiling the diagram of a military mission.

— In this innovative display, Iglesias pays tribute to the CineNic projector, one of the oldest machines in the history of filmmaking. By covering the window in a black film with large triangular perforations, he was able to evoke the flow of light emitted by a projector and allude to the images that ultimately appear on screen.

around an exclusive Nike soccer ball used by a Barcelona team. Such expressions of homage are sometimes reciprocated. In a more cultural exchange, the Girona Museum of Cinema lent Vinçon a collection of vintage projectors for a window display launching a new home-cinema product. A more serious side of window design at Vinçon emerges from the firm's interest in current affairs, a category that included a display expressing solidarity with fishermen affected by the tragedy of Galicia's Prestige oil spills.

A prime example of symbolism in window display is a black leathersofa draped with a spotlit cape, a scene carefully puttogether to evoke images of a snorting bull pawing the dirt

And the war in Iraq prompted the store's plea for peace in the form of an enlarged example of a poem by Octavio Paz. At another time, the window became the stage for a debate between Vinçon and *Avui*, a Catalan newspaper that criticized the store for its lack of novelties. A star product at the time was a small rubber money-

box in the shape of a bulldog. A best-seller, but also an item cited in the newspaper's commentary. Vinçon responded by filling a window with bulldog moneyboxes which appeared to be poring over endless inventories of products in stock.

Witty window displays outside the arena of debate and newsworthy events are those that present bigger-than-life versions of new products. As long ago as the 1970s, Vinçon moved giant coffee mugs out of the shop window and onto the pavement, astonishing passers-by. A more recent display offered onlookers a slice of cutting-edge design in the form of a colossal pair of kitchen shears suspended in the window.

Vinçon's image is conveyed not only by its shop windows, but also by the design of its carrier bags, its product display and the overall 'corporate look'. The result is a retail package tied together with the twine of coherent aesthetics and convincing concepts. In 1972 America Sánchez chose theatrically inspired colours for the store's logo: red and black. And don't look for the pale minimalist look inside either, where brightly spotlit products stand out like jewels against a background of velvety black – a space enveloped in mystery and dotted with eye-catching discoveries. The same dark backdrop extends to the

windows, where boxed-in scenes offer creatively crafted previews of what can be found inside. Vinçon's window displays allow a hint of the inner mystery to escape into the street.

Among the features that distinguish Vinçon from similar shops are its carrier bags. Many well-known graphic artists – such as Javier Mariscal, George Hardy, Pati Núñez and Barbara Kruger – have poured their talents into revamping the bag over

The war in Iraq prompted the store's plea for peace in the form of an enlarged example of a poem by Octavio Paz

the years, turning it into a collector's piece. Here, too, red and black are the preferred colours, together with white and touches of bright primary shades. The bags represent Vinçon's philosophy, says Sergio Amat, in the sense that 'we like to make people think they leave the shop taking a little piece of it with them'. The more than 35 designs that have enhanced these bags to date have even appeared in an exhibition.

Vinçon has cultural value, thanks to its owners' attempts to understand and communicate the meaning of design, and the key to its commercial success lies in these efforts as well. What's more, providing customers with the creative concepts behind each designer object is a sophisticated way of building and maintaining the store's corporate identity.

their pricey merchandise, shield their windows and ward off the angry crowd.

Buenos Aires, Argentina (20 December 2001). A branch of the Banca Nazionale del Lavoro burns after rioters set it on fire during clashes in the city's financial district in Buenos Aires. Argentine Presi-

dent Fernando de la Rua stepped down after thousands of protesters gathered at the Plaza de Mayo square, demanding his resignation.

Tea

Sp

m

irit

Department store Selfridges in London approaches artists, photographers and even magazine editors to create cultural stories for commercial purposes

SELFRIDGES

— From August to October 2003, a display window at Selfridges in London boosts the strong brand concept of Griffin streetwear without relying on the fashions themselves. Interior-design studio El Ultimo Grito, in collaboration with Nathalie de Laval, employs a method known as 'tagging' to showcase the Griffin label. The result is a dynamic statement based on the simple use of vinyl stickers in three colours.

Team Spirit

By REMI ABBAS

LONDON — Since the dawn of the twentieth century, Selfridges has been at the forefront of British department-store shopping. Occupying a block nestled at the top end of London's Oxford Street, it holds a majestic place within the imagination of the consumer. Famed for its explorative window design, Selfridges specializes in windows that extend beyond the physical premises of the store. These windows generate news, bridging the gap between commerce and culture through an ongoing engagement with the artistic and social pursuits that bear the mark of culture.

To ensure a high level of creativity, Selfridges relies on a nonsystematic strategy for window design. The store's Inhouse 3D Creative Team and Creative Direction Department develop themes, but they also draw upon other avenues to infuse their

> *The windows at Selfridges generate news, bridging the gap between commerce and culture*

work with originality. After hatching a collective idea, they commission a carefully selected individual or organization to execute the plan in question. Designers at Selfridges have collaborated with artist Barbara Kruger, ad agency Mother and photographer Rankin, among others.

James Bidwell, marketing director at Selfridges, has overall responsibility for window design. He boasts a career that includes a number of marketing posts, most notably those at Disney and eToys. Past experience makes him well placed to oversee an operation fired by a multidisciplinary approach. 'Either we decide what goes

— In September 2003, Chris Bovill and John Allison of ad agency TBWA win the Creative Futures competition organized by *Creative Review* magazine. As part of the event, the duo move the entire contents of their office into the Selfridges window, where they work for three weeks under the curious gaze of onlookers. Photography by TBWA\London.

in the windows internally, or we collaborate with an external director to create a scheme,' says Bidwell of the window displays, adding that Selfridges sometimes collaborates 'with a museum, a gallery, an artist or even a magazine'. Calling Selfridges 'a hub of creativity', he explains that while his team may not come up with all the ideas, they do provide a stage for the

ment based on the simple use of vinyl stickers in three colours.

57

— Winding down at the end of the day. Bovill and Allison continue to hold client meetings, teach a class and play 'air hockey' every afternoon at three. Photography by TWBA/London

— To create *Refrigerators* for the Feast project (2003 winter-holiday windows), Thomas Rentmeister covered 12 fridges with Penaten baby cream. Courtesy of and photography by Thomas Rentmeister.

— Another display belonging to the Feast project is this array of brightly coloured clay chandeliers by Los Angeles-based artist Pae White: a work of art called *Christmas in July*. Courtesy of Pae White and Greengrassi, London. Photography by Thomas Rentmeister.

— David Batchelor's *Brick Lane Remix* (2003) comprises steel shelving units, light boxes (found and purchased), acrylic sheet, vinyl, polycarbonate, fluorescent lights, cable, plugs and plugboards gathered from a variety of shops. Courtesy of David Batchelor and Wilkinson Gallery, London. Photography by Thomas Rentmeister.

— Anya Gallacio's display centres on six gilded potatoes cast in bronze; she calls the piece, which dates from 2001, *Of the Terrible Doubt of Appearances*. Courtesy of Anya Gallaccio and Thomas Dane, London. Photography by Thomas Rentmeister.

— Gary Hume's window display features a painted bronze snowman coated in enamel (taken from *Snowmen*, a work completed in 2002). The sculpture is 183 centimetres high and 90 centimetres in diameter. Courtesy of Gary Hume and White Cube, London. Photography by Thomas Rentmeister.

He entered shop after shop, priced nothing, spoke no word, and looked at all objects with a wild and vacant stare. Edgar Allen Poe

— American artist Barbara Kruger weaves irony into her 2003 winter-sale display for Selfridges. A good perusal of the window reveals a mild critique of consumerism embedded in philosophical statements, slogans and passages from fiction, including Edgar Allen Poe's 'The Man of the Crowd'.

2003 Christmas display. Having opted to use artists for this particular scenario, Selfridges invited Pablo Lafuente, news editor at *Art Review* magazine, to curate the December windows. Lafuente devised a theme and assembled a group of artists capable of satisfying the client's agenda. 'They wanted people with a certain name, people with good professional experience who could put something together quickly,' Lafuente says of the brief he received. His choices included artists like Gary Hume, Anya Gallacio, Thomas Rentmeister and David Batchelor, all of whom agreed to participate in the project.

Many of these artists liked the idea

Ultimately, Selfridges' window displays are designed to entice customers to enter the store and buy what they find there

of displaying their work in an unconventional setting and were encouraged by the prospect of holiday shoppers interacting with their creations. 'When you work with Selfridges, you have a really big budget,' recalls an enthusiastic Lafuente, 'and five windows in Oxford Street over Christmas time, and 7000 people going into that store every day, which is vast. It was a nice experience.' While recognizing that the work of many contemporary artists bridges art and design, he also notes that such work rarely appears outside a gallery context. Why not exhibit art-cum-design in shop windows, he asks, as well as in other unorthodox spaces?

Although many shared projects have been successful, collaboration between external and retail organizations does have its pitfalls. Window design that may seem firmly rooted in art is nonetheless based on a desire to attract consumer interest. David Batchelor, an artist whose work played a major role in the Feast displays, expresses reservations about the collaborative process. Batchelor's contribution featured a number of light boxes obtained from shops. Dismayed by elements of the presentation of the work, he was especially

expression of others' ideas, working with them to make the end result successful for everyone involved.

Illustrating the process is a joint project between the department store and *Creative Review* magazine. As part of the 2003 Creative Futures event, Chris Bovill and John Allison of TBWA moved the entire contents

of their office into the Selfridges window. The activities of the duo, selected in recognition of their advertising talents, became the window display, as they held meetings, worked on ad campaigns and demonstrated to passers-by their method of working.

Another example of mutually beneficial teamwork is Feast, Selfridges'

of David Batchelor and Wilkinson Gallery, London. Photography by Thomas Rentmeister.

upset by the use of promotional material that obscured a section of his art. At the same time, however, he realizes that the negotiation between artist and shop window is not without risk. 'It's part of the process of dealing with people whose focus is not exactly art. Something always happens that wouldn't happen in a

---

When artists design display windows, 'something always happens that wouldn't happen in a designated art space'.
David Batchelor

---

designated art space,' he says. 'It was frustrating, but understandable. As an artist, there's no point in getting too crazy about it.'

Ultimately, Selfridges' window displays are designed to entice customers to enter the store and buy what they find there. What drives these displays, therefore, is interaction with passing shoppers, which Selfridges generates by making the windows a vessel for cultural commentary – one that hints at a knowledge of shoppers' lives. Barbara Kruger's intelligent critique of consumerism exemplifies this aspect of the displays; the political edge of her message makes the windows more compelling.

This style of message has to appeal

'Windows are playing a role that says, "Engage with us — we are doing innovative things here."'
James Bidwell

---

to a number of audiences. Oxford Street is renowned for the volume of custom it receives. Selfridges catches the eye of a passenger on the top deck of a bus, a curious tourist, a stroller, a businesswoman, a street cleaner; its windows must play to a broad range of viewing perspectives. 'We look at our windows on two levels,' says Bidwell, who distinguishes between 'people passing by who deal with each window on an individual level and those people across the street'. Those

across the street, he notes, need 'a consistency of story'.

Selfridges prides itself on an ability to portray stories that stir up interest across the board. The window as story generator typifies the hybrid nature of the store's communicative displays. Selfridges offers theatre, shopping and reality TV – invigorating its windows by tapping into culture while also being part of that culture. According to Bidwell, a sense of anticipation accompanies the development of a window scheme. In mentioning bus passengers on their way to and from work, who clearly have 'a sense of en-

gagement', he says: 'Everyone knows the product inside the store. The point is to get people to engage with 'Selfridges the brand and Selfridges the look.' Windows are playing a role that says, 'Engage with us – we are doing innovative things here.'

Pablo Lafuente agrees. He says that many people remember going to see the windows at Selfridges as children, because the displays were simply something that had to be seen. His comment emphasizes the significance of Selfridges' windows as cultural events that have helped shape a nation of shoppers.

very public art gallery™   THE ART AUCTION WHERE YOU NOD WITH YOUR MOBILE

Painting
not in use

Paintings for Recycling

Tim Willoughby

— In the spring of 2003, Brit Art and Mother use the windows at Selfridges as a gallery space for the exhibition of art. The project represents a first in the world of art: an auction that invites window-shoppers to bid on works of art via the text-messaging function of their mobile phones. *Painting Not in Use*, a work by Tim Willoughby, is one of the pieces at the public sale.

winter of love

Ron Broomfield
Gnome Collector

Ron Broomfield has been collecting gnomes for over 40 years, and his entire house and garden is dedicated to them. He shares his home in the Lincolnshire market town of Alford with over 1000 gnomes. "Gnomes have become my life," he said, so much so that he has four gnome outfit in which he dresses. Ron uses his hobby to raise money for the NSPCC.

www.selfridges.com

I: 08708 377 377

— A shop window included in Selfridges' 2002 Christmas campaign, The Winter of Love, showcases Ron Broomfield's gnome collection. Broomfield, who has collected gnomes for over 40 years, shares his home with over 1000 of the legendary creatures.

— Featured in the multifaceted Feast project is Mark Barnett's life-size chocolate sculpture of cookery queen Nigella Lawson. Barnett spent two weeks crafting this work of art, which helps to promote an in-store book signing by Britain's 'domestic goddess'.

— Nike's 28 windows portray a visual language that conveys to perfection the perpetual motion of 90 minutes of football play. On display are Brazilian and Portuguese national uniforms, Nike footwear and the Aerow Total 90 ball. Photography by Remco Vloon.

n for
angle
dless
y by

— Nike takes a kaleidoscopic approach to its April 2004 theme, Nike Football 2004: Product in Perpetual Motion for 90 Minutes. To create a fusion of unceasing motion and images, the photographer shot the product through a triangle of mirrored surfaces. In a third interpretation of the theme, mirror-clad towers and graphic backdrops create endless reflections. Numbers on the window symbolize the 90 minutes of regulation play in a football match. Photography by Remco Vroom

— In May 2002, a programme of themed events at Selfridges – 23 1/2 Days of Bollywood – generates window displays filled with the drama, colour and glamour of Indian cinema. Windows taking their cue from traditional advertising for popular Bollywood films promote movies such as *Kabhi, Khushi, Khadbie Gham* (K3G) and *Devdas*.

— A collaborative project developed by Selfridges and Channel 4 draws a link between Bollywood and test cricket, a concept illustrating the dramatic tension present in both Indian cinema and cricket matches between England and India.

most
ves a
comes
sumes
ndows
limit-
act re-
urish-
alike,
rs can
If, at
ce of
ism,
alm
self.
take
nif-
may
ne.

Reuters/WFA

Montreal, Canada (28 July 2003). A window is smashed at a Gap store in downtown Montreal, where protesters have gathered to disrupt three days of World Trade Organization meetings. Attended by 25 trade ministers, the meetings are an attempt to find common ground on issues of farm subsidies and medicine for poorer countries.

Material

By CHARLOTTE VAUDREY
Photography by
STEFANO PANDINI

Most shoppers hit Milan with finely honed must-have lists, surely none of which includes the extraordinary items topping lists drawn up by Moschino window designer JoAnn Tan, a longtime resident of Italy's fashion capital. From tracking down 1500 feather butterflies – and a glue gun – to finding four and a half tonnes of red, second-hand clothing, the Art Institute of Chicago graduate is always on the alert for potential props, especial-

mag, Tan happ
which she woul
and sew to her h
and spaniel-sha
waiting for a faci
sion from a story
extensions are
women's prison i
a line providing
who 'had the stor

*Franco M
renowne
pot shots
crowd, bot
and th

Evidence

l upon the hair,
ter wrap around
nade dachshund-
cushions, while
ecoiling in revul-
ging Posh Spice's
urced from a
oscow, Tan spied
vebsite for those
h to read on'. She

hino was
r taking
he fashion
he makers
earers

man renowned for taking pot shots at the fashion crowd, both the makers and the wearers. After launching his label in 1983, Moschino became the original *enfant terrible* of the fashion industry. In a field where opinions are frowned upon for fear of spooking customers, Moschino made social commentary part of the company's personality, aggressively addressing AIDS and decrying drug addiction and government corruption. His irreverence towards the fashion establishment led to copyright battles with Chanel, among others, after he spoofed the label's perfume by splashing 'Channel No 5' across Moschino T-shirts. An iconoclast, he claimed

Parodying fashion and those obsessed by it, shop windows conceived by JoAnn Tan for Moschino have a democratic appeal: from children passing with parents to streetwise scooter kids and art critics, everybody has an opinion

MOSCHINO

— Above and next spread: a recurring Moschino theme that Tan relishes playing on is that of the fashion victim. For Crocodiles, a literal interpretation of the Peter Pan theme of the Spring/Summer 2000 collection, she combined painted foam-rubber reptiles with leggings and boots from the collection.

74

Material Evidence

By CHARLOTTE VAUDREY
Photography by
STEFANO PANDINI

Most shoppers hit Milan with finely honed must-have lists, surely none of which includes the extraordinary items topping lists drawn up by Moschino window designer JoAnn Tan, a longtime resident of Italy's fashion capital. From tracking down 1500 feather butterflies – and a glue gun – to finding four and a half tonnes of red, second-hand clothing, the Art Institute of Chicago graduate is always on the alert for potential props, especially those that can be ordered in bulk. 'I'll squirrel away the source,' she says, 'and when an appropriate theme comes up, I'll be, like, turkey feathers!'

Called Hairpets, Tan's display in Moschino's flagship store at the time of writing comprises pouty mannequins whose hair grows, Picasso-like, into lapdogs to be petted and stroked. Flipping through a gossip mag, Tan happened upon the hair, which she would later wrap around and sew to her handmade dachshund- and spaniel-shaped cushions, while waiting for a facial. Recoiling in revulsion from a story alleging Posh Spice's extensions are sourced from a women's prison in Moscow, Tan spied a line providing a website for those who 'had the stomach to read on'. She

---

Franco Moschino was renowned for taking pot shots at the fashion crowd, both the makers and the wearers

---

pounced on the address, ordered synthetic samples and was able to take the irony-infused project to its conclusion.

Hairpets is Tan's comment on vanity and the exaggeration of it. The display continues the approach taken by brand founder Franco Moschino, a man renowned for taking pot shots at the fashion crowd, both the makers and the wearers. After launching his label in 1983, Moschino became the original *enfant terrible* of the fashion industry. In a field where opinions are frowned upon for fear of spooking customers, Moschino made social commentary part of the company's personality, aggressively addressing AIDS and decrying drug addiction and government corruption. His irreverence towards the fashion establishment led to copyright battles with Chanel, among others, after he spoofed the label's perfume by splashing 'Channel No 5' across Moschino T-shirts. An iconoclast, he claimed that 'fashion is something you can laugh about forever', especially because 'people take it so seriously'. One of the principles of Moschino-think is 'Fantasy starts where duty stops', a maxim that Kuala Lumpur-born Tan embraces. As a student she had avidly followed the advertising campaigns, which Moschino himself devised. 'I thought the fact that the ads were nothing to do with fashion-

— Franco Moschino used the theatre-box window (350w x 250d x 360h cm) in the flagship boutique on Via Sant'Andrea to broadcast opinions and subvert traditional images. Featured here is JoAnn Tan's creation, a tacky hair salon where mannequins read gossip magazine *Hola* while getting their hair set, a scene that ties in with the Spanish theme of the Spring/Summer 2001 collection. Photography by Santi Caleca.

— A
Croc
ed fo

— Above and next spread: during the photo shoot for Flat People, a window display starring card-thin cutouts of models refusing drink, Tan made sure that front and rear photographs of each model would match, when cut out, by having both model and photographer take exactly the same positions for each new shot.

— Indicating the extent of Tan's freedom to do her own thing, projects like Hairpets (above), which features clothing, shoes and sunglasses from Moschino Spring/Summer 2004 collection, alternate with others, like Flat People (pages 75, 76 and 77), which display no actual merchandise at all.

hing,
s 75,

— Hairpets, a comment on vanity and its exaggeration, is a surrealist flight of imagination à la Picasso. Tan wrapped her handmade dachshund- and spaniel-shaped cushions in the same synthetic hair that sprouts from ultra-long-haired wigs by Il Parruccaio di Milano.

was just brilliant,' she recalls. Crafting his own window displays until 1993, Moschino used the theatre-box window in the boutique on Via Sant'Andrea as a means of communication, broadcasting his moods and opinions and subverting traditional images. Architect Fabio Novembre calls the Moschino windows 'a landmark in the fashion system'. Tan affirms, adding that 'the strongest style came from Moschino himself, not from those who worked on the windows after he'd passed away. Moschino's was definitely the act to follow.'

JoAnn Tan and Franco Moschino never met face to face. When Tan approached the fashion house for a

In the quest for the gobsmackingly got-to-stop-and-look display, JoAnn Tan undertakes gruellingly labour-intensive tasks

position as a trainee, the onset of AIDS had already prevented Franco from coming to the studio. The current director of Moschino, Rosella Jardini, relates that although the company rarely takes on trainees, she was so struck by the diminutive Malaysian's work that she felt compelled to discuss Tan with Moschino. Jardini describes a dress Tan designed while studying for her degree in film, cartoon animation and fashion. The sleeves of the silk frock were in the form of jugs tilted to suggest a flow of milk pouring from their spouts. Jardini says the work made Franco laugh. With the stamp of approval from number one, the newly graduated Tan was hired. In due course she rose from trainee to fashion assistant, a position that evolved into her responsibilities as head of the Cheap and Chic line, the apex in a young fashion designer's career. Fresh from her promotion, however, Tan became captivated by window-dressing. She found herself yearning to blend visual commercial communication with modern installation art. Her pitch to Jardini included the use of mirrors that would allow the passer-by to catch her reflection wearing one of the outfits displayed. Jardini, long delighted by Tan's work, gave the 26-year-old the nod.

— In creating the irony-infused Hairpets, Tan develops the approach taken by brand founder Franco Moschino.

To begin with, Tan ran her ideas past Jardini, but that formality was soon dropped. Essentially, Tan had carte blanche from the outset. Grinning, she describes 'Moschino's display of a giant egg with a smiley face one Easter – with not a scrap of the collection included'. The acceptance of this unprecedented concept was her assurance 'that I would have a free rein'.

Initially, there was no question of Tan choosing between her two roles. Working long days, she relied heavily

— Christmas Trees, appearing in a window of a former Moschino store, presents knitwear, satin handbags, suede shoes and umbrellas, all in various shades of green. Items are from the Moschino Cheap and Chic and the Moschino Jeans Autumn/Winter 2001/2002 collections.

on found objects to fabricate a monthly window display, while still designing the line. From amassing beige high heels from the collection and standing them neatly on the floor in the 'boot' shape of Italy to envisaging a heap of discarded clothing (and four and a half tonnes of it at that) as full skirts for materialistic mannequins, Tan proved herself inventive and resourceful from day one. After a year and a half of juggling deadlines though, Tan ruefully remembers that 'it got to the stage where I had stopped sleeping and I had no life'. With more ideas for window displays than her clothing line, she ac-

'When I hear the whisper of an idea, I have to sit quietly by myself to chase it.'
JoAnn Tan

knowledged that her heart was lost to installation and made the obvious choice. Suddenly blessed with an extra eight hours a day, Tan started building the installations that would take her displays to the next level.

While she looks to Franco Moschino's windows to set the tone for her own, Tan's work reflects an evolution of the original aesthetic. In the quest for the perfectly finished, gobsmackingly got-to-stop-and-look display, Tan undertakes gruellingly labour-intensive tasks, like the gluing of 1500 feather butterflies, one by one. Her ability to infuse ordinary objects with a tangible spirit has resulted in gangs of boys screeching their scooters to a halt to gawk at a dress encircled by scissors spiralling from the ceiling: their blades yawning open, tools used by workaday seamstresses became a menacing swarm. An integral aspect of Tan's progressive approach lies in work that often borders on the conceptual, as illustrated by the figure of a mannequin shaped from cotton wool to resemble a human cloud.

Having contributed to collections that required her to predict what would work up to a year in advance, Tan considers the 30-day turnaround for window display a luxury. She gives herself a week to think through the concept, start sourcing materials and decide whether she and assistant Sarah Cave, a technical production

specialist, can assemble the display themselves. Tan devises the concepts alone: 'When I hear the whisper of an idea, I have to sit quietly by myself to chase it.' The remaining 20 days are spent tracking down materials and constructing the necessary parts. 'A lot of the time I'm sewing while

A considerable amount of Tan's work hinges on the fashion victim, making Milan the ideal location for her studio

Sarah's welding,' says Tan of installation builds. Tan's ingenious use of materials means her work often strays into a surrealist realm. In Pasta People, a tongue-in-cheek window, Tan and Cave spent two days boiling pasta to craft three busts. Tan admits that she and Cave 'definitely went beyond ourselves with that one' and that she still can't eat spaghetti.

A considerable amount of Tan's work hinges on the fashion victim, making Milan the ideal location for

— Christmas Trees employs seasonal decorations made completely from pieces in the Moschino collection.

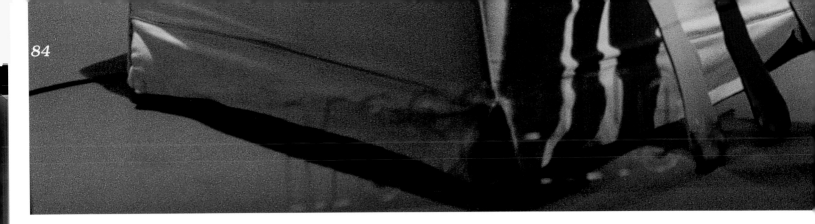

— Above and right: the sheared-in-half dress in Half a Window, part of the Spring/Summer 2002 collection, was adapted for this display by Bonaveri Manichini. Half a Window started out as a simple experiment to test the possibility of creating only half a window. Second-hand, sawed-in-half furniture was staged by Scenart.

her studio, which is festooned in a plethora of Polaroid shots. 'I have research material everywhere,' she admits. In her Flat People display, which features card-thin cutouts of models refusing drink, Tan wryly comments on fashion's preoccupation with skinniness. 'What better way,' crystallizes local architect Sean Dix, 'to

'Tan's work is quirky, witty and hugely imaginative.'
Manolo Blahnik

communicate the lack of depth of the fashion obsessed.' Tan's approach goes beyond the aesthetic: her consideration of the mechanics of movement is evident from the card figures' quasi-realistic poses.

Cocking a snook at fashion's fixation on über-tall models in a display called Long Legged Ladies, Tan gave mannequins triple-length legs, caricaturing fashion illustrations. Standing next to one of her leggy creations, Tan reached only waist height. Bringing in skills acquired at college, Tan and Cave sculpted then painted new, excessively long legs for the mannequins which Scenart, the scenographers who stage the sets at La Scala, had rough-cast in Styrofoam. Up close, the limbs are anatomically detailed, adding to the degree of optical distortion.

Tan discovered from experience what works by seeing the kinds of visuals that stop people in their tracks. 'Obviously, the eye-grabbing element has to be there, but more is needed, so your mind stops for a second to digest it.' What she's after are 'levels that appeal to children and levels that strike someone from the design industry', all in the same window. One display drew enthusiastic raves from passer-by Manolo Blahnik even as it was being installed. 'When I'm in

Milan I go to Via Sant'Andrea specifically to see the Moschino windows,' says the famed shoe designer, who calls Tan's work 'quirky, witty and hugely imaginative'. He and Tan have much in common, since the pattern-making technique taught in Tan's shoemaking studies is a skill regularly used to create her 'really weird shapes'.

Self-depreciating to the last, Tan grudgingly nominates her favourite window as one featuring a male mannequin fashioned from stapled-together card cutouts of musical notes

> *'Sometimes I consciously set out to provoke, and sometimes it's a happy accident.'*
> *JoAnn Tan*

– the dashing partner of a female mannequin dancing in the window. Romantic and poetic, the scene was a popular display that drew many onlookers, according to the designer.

Tan is currently interested in the reaction of people to windows of all kinds: from cute to thoughtful to horrendously gross. 'I don't mind that some people see Hairpets as being quite creepy,' she discloses, referring to her latest design. 'Sometimes I consciously set out to provoke, and sometimes it's just a happy accident.' She says that in each design, whether an intricately assembled environment or a grand gesture, 'being provocative is an important aspect of making people stop – even if simply to say, "Wow! Look at all those butterflies." It's all connected to marketing and to making Moschino stand out, which draws customers in.' Part merchandising and part installation art, Tan's displays exude the vibrancy of film stills carefully extracted from a longer story.

— Long Legged Ladies caricatures fashion illustrations. Tan sculpted and then painted triple-length legs, which Sce-nart had roughcast in Styrofoam.

— Tan crafted peacocks from material used in the Precollection Autumn/Winter 2003/2004, replacing their ostentatious ta
with dresses made of the same fabric. Tan's inventive approach surfaces in the birds' feet, which are constructed from bent wi
wrapped in ribbon.

— Much of Tan's work borders on the conceptual, as illustrated by Cloud Person, a cotton-wool mannequin resembling a human cloud. Clouds by Scenart set the stage for theatrically dramatic lighting. The dress is from the Moschino Spring/Summer 2002 collection.

— Taking centre stage in January 2004 was Ice Queen, a reference to 'that kind of woman'. Made of cast resin and produced by Kobe, the chilly display features a jacket from the Moschino Precollection Spring/Summer 2004.

— Monsters in the Closet alludes to the common fear of something hideous hiding in the wardrobe. Tan tucked a cube covered in faux fur set with Plexiglas 'eyes' into a heap of clothes from the Moschino Spring/Summer 2003 collection. Adding a sinister glow to the scene is a series of tiny red bulbs set behind blackout cloth.

— The coat, trousers, sunglasses and shoes seen in Clotheshorse are from the Moschino Autumn/Winter 2002/2003 collection. The star of Clotheshorse has been constructed from a tubular metal frame mounted on a pedestal (hidden by sand), shaped with bubble wrap and provided with a final layer of brown and dun-coloured second-hand clothing.

ss — Above and next page: Tan often undertakes gruellingly labour-intensive tasks; to create Butterflies, a window loose-ly based on the concept of attraction, she carefully glued, one by one, 1500 feather butterflies sourced from a

Scandinavian supplier. The dress is from the Moschino Precollection Autumn/Winter 2002/2003.

— A gift-wrapped Styrofoam dinosaur fills the window in Christmas Present, an appropriately seasonal display. Dress and shoes are from the Moschino Autumn/Winter 2003/2004 collection.

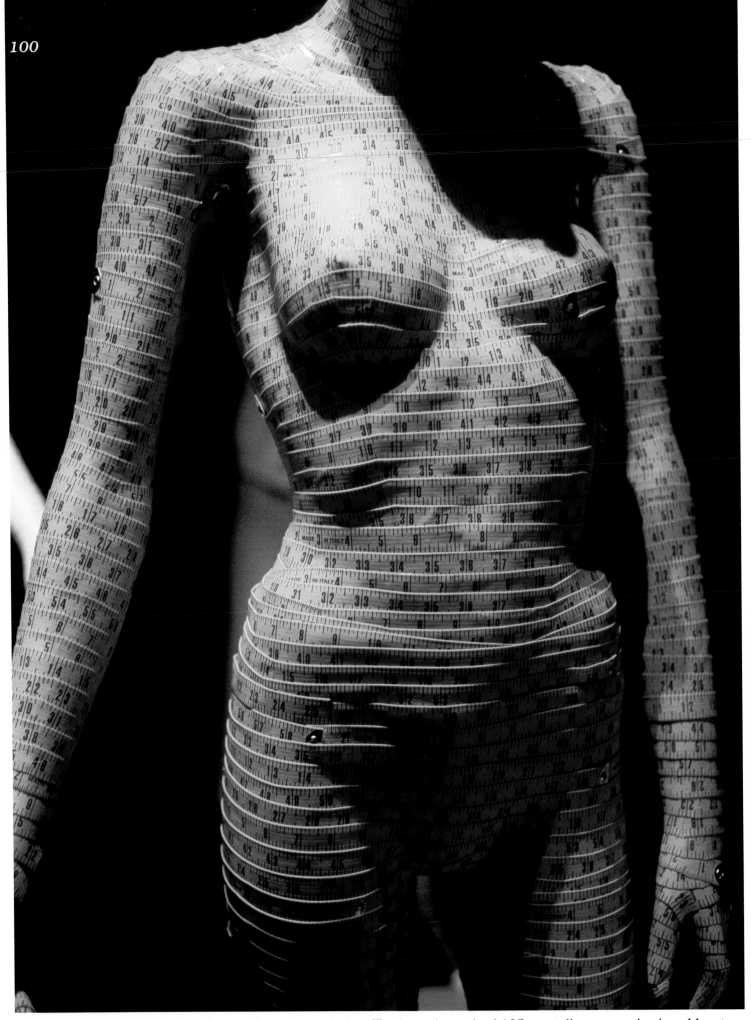

— Tape Measure People parodies an obsession with size. Tan bound standard 185-cm-tall mannequins in rubber tape measures. Seemingly straightforward, the process actually necessitated the painstaking clipping of tiny triangular segments along each length of tape to ensure that each strip hugged the mannequins' contours.

— Coinciding with a celebration of the Moschino label's 20th anniversary, Music Note Man is a mannequin fashioned from stapled-together card cutouts of musical notes; he materializes as a human form of the music played by a vintage gramophone. Dress and shoes are from the Moschino Autumn/Winter 2003/2004 collection.

0 x 120 cm.

eyes of

Buenos Aires, Argentina (19 December 2001). Looters take goods from a Buenos Aires supermarket amid a cloud of tear gas. The Argentine government has declared a state of siege, giving officials the

thority to confront acts of looting and violence that have left four people dead and hundreds ured.

ONT

Theater

of Sales

By CHRIS SC
Photography
STÉPHANE MU

PARIS — The name I
immediately brings to m
luxury, class, craftsn
refinement. Further e
firm's impeccable imag

For the successful launch of a window display for 319 stores worldwide, the team at Louis Vuitton goes to work on the scenario six to seven months in advance

LOUIS VUITTON

Theater of Sales

— Following an initial briefing, American theatre-man Bob Wilson handed over two simple pencil drawings, along with Pantone colour references, and told Valérie Cazals and her team to 'go with it'. His graphic treatment of the company logo turned out to be so strong and dynamic that it developed into a leather-goods project. In this window at the Champ Elysées shop in Paris, selected menswear and shoes from LV's Autumn/Winter 2002/2003 ready-to-wear collection are not overwhelmed by the fussiness often seen in over-crowded Christmas displays.

By CHRIS SCOTT
Photography by
STÉPHANE MURATET

PARIS — The name Louis Vuitton immediately brings to mind a world of luxury, class, craftsmanship and refinement. Further enhancing the firm's impeccable image are window displays beautifully and precisely executed, frequently with an amusing or unusual touch. They originate at the Paris headquarters, where Director of Merchandising Valérie Cazals and her team oversee the design of window displays for Louis Vuitton's 319 (and rising) stores worldwide. Each outlet boasts between two and 15 windows, which are changed at least six times a year: a major operation, especially in view of LV's strong brand image, which is reinforced by a myriad of messages conveyed throughout the year. These are dictated largely by new products, promotions, seasons and shows, but also by numerous rules, requirements and global calendar constraints.

Having only one brand to promote allows less freedom than that enjoyed by department stores or other establishments with a variety of brands to display. Creativity at Louis Vuitton does not appear to be stifled, however, by the obvious restrictions. Above all, LV's window designers aim for clarity of communication, preferably without sending too many messages at one time. 'What do we want to talk about?' is the recurring question. 'The windows have to talk to *you*,' replies Cazals, 'and hopefully communicate on an emotional level.'

Gaston-Louis Vuitton, grandson of founder Louis Vuitton, voiced his theoretical and practical views on display in 1925. 'It is all about attracting and selling,' he wrote. 'Display is the art of presenting something to sell in a way that brings out a desire to buy and allows the sale to happen.' He fully understood the importance of lighting: 'Lighting is going to give you shadow, to modify the value and colour of what you are showing. It appears to me that lighting, as used in the theatre, could render a remarkable service. It is a

— Japanese sculptor and manga artist Takashi Murakami supplied Cazals and her team with basic concepts and the freedom to develop these ideas. The joint venture led to a window that includes Murakami's 'Eye Love Monogram' bag, the brightly coloured Louis Vuitton logo and, on the glass itself, the artist's distinctive drawings.

never-ending resource, which needs to be researched.' Cazals totally agrees with Vuitton's original thinking; the same rules still both players and stage have to be well lit.

Cazals works with a core team of three designers and a global team of around 25 people, plus a dozen or so regular freelancers with whom she has built up contacts over the years. But she remains open to the potential represented by new artists, designers, scenographers, creative computer people and input from any number of

---

'Lighting is going to give you shadow, to modify the value and colour of what you are showing.'
Gaston-Louis Vuitton (1925)

---

areas. 'You have to be open,' she stresses. Restrictions notwithstanding, team members have a great deal of expressive freedom, even more than in-store designers. Fortunately, budget issues, which may emerge later, do not interfere with the creative process. Cazals wants the designers to be extremely free in what they propose, not weighed down by limitations. 'Having to launch within a box is the only constraint,' she says, adding that a vital part of the design process is 'sending them off to play'.

Working with artists such as American theatre-man Robert Wilson and Japanese sculptor and manga artist Takashi Murakami has proved to be very successful. Both artists provided the team with basic concepts and the freedom to develop these ideas, and both were open to the team's suggestions. This atmosphere of mutual respect brought about excellent results. Following an initial briefing, Bob

— Light, colour and an interesting composition of products and display materials are essential to the appeal of this window. The colour blue creates a crisp, aloof ambience, and the background colour provides an ideal context for the items on display, which correspond beautifully to their surroundings.

— March/April 2003: Inspired by the vanishing act of the slithery chameleon, LV's design team camouflages leather goods by placing them against a background that replicates their motif.

— Products in Murakami's Champs Elysées window – Cherry Blossom and leather goods bearing the monograms Vernis Fuchsia and 'Eye Love Monogram' – are every bit as 'cute' (to use a term heard in many a Japanese boutique) as the design on the backdrop.

Wilson handed over two simple pencil drawings, along with Pantone colour references, and told the team to 'go with it'. His graphic treatment of the company logo turned out to be so strong and dynamic that it developed into a leather-goods project. And in the winter of 2002, Wilson's neon colours and graphic lines spilled 'out of the box' onto the pavement, a first for Louis Vuitton windows, as well as into the store, a welcome change from the dominant reds and greens of the Christmas season. Murakami's contribution followed a different course. His colourful monogram for leather goods ultimately evolved into window displays that integrated the Murakami mind-set with the world of

Louis Vuitton, a combination that led to fresh, fun windows.

Coming up with ideas is never a problem, Cazals insists, nor are the logistics of transmitting them worldwide. Communication between Paris and all points on LV's global network

---

Following an initial briefing, Bob Wilson handed over two simple pencil drawings, along with Pantone colour references, and told the team to 'go with it'

---

is excellent. The most difficult part of the operation comes four to five months before the launch of a new window. Taking place at that time is the presentation of proposals to the *Comité de Validation*, the top management, a group that includes Bernard Arnault, chairman and CEO of LVMH, the corporation that owns Louis Vuitton. 'Preparing for the committee is an art,' says Cazals, who considers the presentation of proposals essential to the success of her work. If the ideas draw no more than a lukewarm response, or are rejected, the ever-enthusiastic and optimistic director of merchandising blames it on a poor presentation. She immediately analyses and dissects the events of the

— In the winter of 2002, Bob Wilson's neon colours and graphic lines spilled 'out of the box' onto the pavement of the Champs Elysées, as well as into the store. The display makes a welcome change from the dominant reds and greens of the Christmas season.

— Featured in Wilson's Christmas window is a wall of vintage trunks, one of which is big enough to transport a dancer. A detail imbued with theatrical drama.

390€

LOUIS VUITTON

— The team's well-ordered 'chandelier window' includes a jacket from the Spring/Summer 2003 ready-to-wear collection and a Louis Vuitton Monogram suitcase that can be opened on two sides.

— The neighbouring window, turned to chaos by a fallen chandelier, presents items from the Spring/Summer 2003 ready-to-wear menswear collection and Damier leather goods.

— Kicking off its 150th anniversary in 2004, Louis Vuitton introduced the 'neon' window, with walls displaying a graphic rendering of a gentleman's portrait. Hardly anyone realized that the gentleman depicted in flashy neon lights was the firm's founder, Monsieur Louis Vuitton.

— A combination of flowers by Murakami and the brightly coloured LV logo makes a perfect setting for the 2003 Spring Collection.

day, looking for reasons, turning negative feedback into a positive factor. The committee's opinion and eventual approval make the outcome of her efforts feel like a collective decision.

Despite reservations among its members, however, sometimes the committee is willing to take a risk. A good example is the 'chandelier project', which resulted in a window display that certainly grabbed the attention of passers-by. One perfectly orderly window contained chandelier,

The most difficult part of the operation comes four to five months before the launch of a new window: the presentation of proposals to the Comité de Validation, the top management

table and chairs, while the one next to it was reduced to total chaos. The chandelier had crashed to the ground. Had it fallen? Was it an accident? Such a mess! And why were the carpet and chair now up on the wall?

Once a project has been approved, the team can concentrate on technical aspects and production can begin. Each new window display requires a period of preparation that lasts six to seven months. Providing hundreds of stores with newly designed windows

— Murakami's colourful monogram for leather goods evolved into window displays that integrated the Murakami mind-set with the world of Louis Vuitton, a combination that led to fresh, fun windows. A great example is the display of items from the Spring/Summer 2003 collection, as seen here in the window on the Champs Elysées.

— May/June 2003: Louis Vuitton's eye-catching windows represent a complete contrast in mood. In one perfectly ordered scene, chandelier, table and chairs create a serene setting, whereas the other half of the twin display has been reduced to total chaos.

— January 2003: The team used polished metals stripes with a lacquered finish to express his Reflect theme. Mirrored over and over again in the shiny surfaces are women's accessories and shoes (Spring/Summer 2003 collection), as well as the gleam of lights illuminating the display.

means creating thousands of mini theatres. An enormous undertaking. Accompanying each new theme is a 100-page (or more), full-colour merchandising manual. Packed with pictures, it works better than words. The manual details how different windows – depending on shape, size, position, location and store classification – should look. Stores fall into categories from A to E, rankings that relate to size, location and which ranges of the brand are carried. An A store carries only one range, while an E outlet, referred to as a 'star' store in a top location, offers customers the entire LV product range. The book is dispatched one week in advance of the changeover, props having been shipped one month earlier. Worldwide, all LV windows change within the same week.

Stressing that details are the hardest thing to control, Cazals admits her obsession with this problem. 'You can

'You can talk theatre, lighting, magic, but if the detail is not just right, the effect is lost. All the effort is in vain.'
Valerie Cazals

talk theatre, lighting, magic, but if the detail is not just right, the effect is lost. All the effort is in vain.' Though perhaps not aware of it, window-shoppers sense that something's wrong at some level or another.

Kicking off its 150th anniversary in 2004, Louis Vuitton introduced the 'neon' window, a concept tested at events and launches throughout the previous year, with walls displaying a graphic rendering of a gentleman's portrait. Owing to its success, the idea was adapted and translated into neon for LV's store windows. Hardly anyone realized that the gentleman depicted in flashy neon lights was the firm's founder, Monsieur Louis Vuitton.

— Another of the design team's chameleon-inspired windows is this 1-by-1-metre space featuring shoes and leather goods.

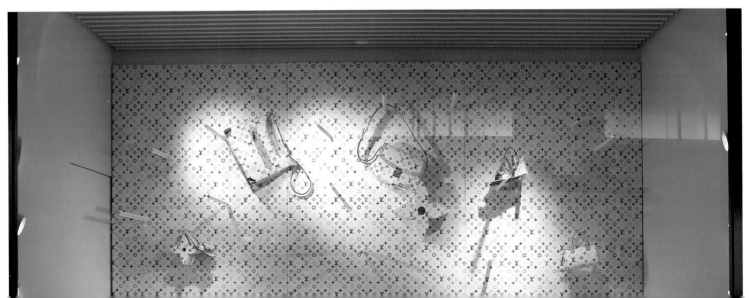

— In a larger window at Galeries Lafayette, leather goods are attached to the background, where they seem to merge into the patterned surface.

Cultur

Text by REMI ABBAS
Photography by
MICHAEL TAYLOR

LONDON — Located on the corner of Sloane Street, overlooking Knightsbridge, Harvey Nichols exudes detached class. As a premier fashion emporium, its style harks back to a golden retail era. Wreathed in an aura

e Club

play windows for over 20 years, steadily progressing through a number of retail outfits. It is at Harvey Nichols, however, that she feels she is at the apogee of window design. 'It's the freedom that you get,' she explains.

Harvey Nichols boasts longstanding relationships among staff members. Wardley, who has been there for over eight years, believes it's the longevity of these alliances that ensures the strength of their designs. At Harvey

Dwarfing passers-by, Harvey Nichols' tall, wide windows transcend the concept of displays to become spectacles of the imagination

HARVEY NICHOLS

Culture Club

Text by REMI ABBAS
Photography by
MICHAEL TAYLOR

LONDON — Located on the corner of Sloane Street, overlooking Knightsbridge, Harvey Nichols exudes detached class. As a premier fashion emporium, its style harks back to a golden retail era. Wreathed in an aura of affluence and exclusivity, Harvey Nichols appeals to the coterie in the know. Elitist without being inaccessible, the establishment wears a mantle of gentility that separates it from other department stores – a sense of chic clearly conveyed by the window displays. Winner of a D&AD award in 1998 for a design created in collaboration with Thomas Heatherwick, Harvey Nichols presents windows that transcend the concept of displays to become spectacles of the imagination.

Headed by Janet Wardley, the store's visual merchandising controller, the window-design team operates with little interference from the board. Wardley has been dressing display windows for over 20 years, steadily progressing through a number of retail outfits. It is at Harvey Nichols, however, that she feels she is at the apogee of window design. 'It's the freedom that you get,' she explains.

Harvey Nichols boasts longstanding relationships among staff members. Wardley, who has been there for over eight years, believes it's the longevity of these alliances that ensures the strength of their designs. At Harvey Nichols, window design is a democratic process; input from a variety of areas is encouraged. This non-hierarchical approach is engendered by the board's willingness to allow creative freedom. 'Windows depend on how innovative the people are who commission the project,' says Thomas Heatherwick. 'With the Harvey Nichols project, we were given an open brief. We weren't led by a strong strategy.' He much appreciated receiving what he calls 'the space to respond'.

Freed from corporate constraints and boardroom demands, the window-design team has little interface with other departments. Instead, aware of the company message, they take direction from a more nebulous place:

— Thomas Heatherwick's Modern Sculpture display weaves in and out of Harvey Nichols' windows. Featured in September 1997, this bold, prizewinning sculpture dominates the pavement area surrounding the store. Photography by Steve Speller.

the cultural environment. Collabora-   dow designers adopt a very different

— Summer 2003: A mannequin picks flowers from a tree in a scheme show-casing warm-weather apparel.

— Minki Balinki's colourful buttons compose a polka-dot backdrop for a mannequin poised to enter the Christmas season in style.

— A Dior display features a tangle of yellow tubing and two wooden figures who threaten to become caught in the snarled lines.

— Tape measures as streamers and masses of ribbons as headdresses: Harvey Nichols proves that even simple attributes from the haberdashery make brilliant Christmas decorations.

— November 2003: View of the colourful Christmas Decoration windows on the corner of Sloane Street.

— Above and next page bottom: Stretch, a September 2003 display, is punctuated by bright, kite-like shapes both outside and inside the window. The colourful, eye-catching forms refer to the flexible, elastic materials so popular in contemporary fashion design.

— Christmas Decoration 2003: Detail of a huge zip revealing three sombrely dressed mannequins

the cultural environment. Collaboration is rare at Harvey Nichols; when they do work with an outsider, they tend to be drawn by talent rather than name or stature. Their choice is invariably someone who can create and steer an appealing narrative. 'We're

'We're not looking to sell the merchandise; we're looking to make a statement.'
Janet Wardley

not looking to sell the merchandise,' says Wardley. 'We're looking to make a statement … push boundaries … do something eye-catching.'

To mention Harvey Nichols is to tap into an instant source of conversation. It's no wonder that artists are eager to meet with Wardley for an exchange of ideas. 'Lots of up-and-coming artists come to see our work,' she says. 'We see what they do, and they pick up on our thoughts.'

Wardley and her team generate ideas through different avenues. One way is by accompanying the store's

buyers to fashion shows, where window designers adopt a very different observation process than do those who are there to buy. Removing themselves from the minutiae of fashion, window designers seek a macro understanding of cultural trends by gauging the influences that inspired the collections. Analyzing culture in this way allows them to create a narrative that relates as much to fashion as it does to contemporary culture. They translate their ideas into window displays.

Windows the size of those at Harvey Nichols provide an opportunity to make a big impression. Each is an imposing expanse – tall and wide, they dwarf passers-by. The sheer magnitude invites designers to delve into themes, to entice the viewer and to usher in a tableau of meanings.

In 1997 Thomas Heatherwick installed a monumental, ribbon-like structure of plywood and polystyrene. Weaving in and out of the 60-metre-long glazed front, it climbed 10 metres up the façade before sweeping back into the interior through openings in the windows. 'I wanted to draw attention to the building itself,' says Heatherwick. 'I chose to treat the glass as if it wasn't even there. Instead

— Student Bruce Morgan contributed to the Strings display, in which fluorescent tubes of yellow rubber extend across the windows, sometimes appearing to penetrate surrounding walls. Jointed wooden mannequins pull and stretch the flexible lines, adding to the animated vitality of the scene.

— Christmas Decoration 2003: A huge zip opens to reveal three sombrely dressed mannequins standing in a sea of oversized 'pearls': a stark contrast to the dazzling colours appearing elsewhere in the holiday windows.

— The Christmas Decoration window bursts with the dynamism of a huge exploding Christmas cracker, evoking a charged sense of excitement. Design specialists Minki Balinki built this visual metaphor.

— Christmas Decoration uses a variety of themes to convey the celebratory feel of the holiday season. Paper chains, a compact tree and a warm, rosy backdrop offset the ethereal look of a levitating mannequin.

— Made of MDF and polystyrene, bright shapes and a colourful table craft an illusion of play and lightness, reinforced by a cheerful dash of kitsch.

of creating 12 different window displays, I wondered if it was possible to do one thing that would connect the place together.'

Part of the allure of these windows lies in the past. Heritage is a key element in the Harvey Nichols' mystique. Melding history with contemporary life, levelling the tense relationship between old and new, between nostalgia and modernity, Harvey Nichols treads lightly between past and present without succumbing

Removing themselves from the minutiae of fashion, Harvey Nichols' window designers seek a macro understanding of cultural trends by gauging the influences that inspired the collections

to either. In so doing, the store enjoys the patronage of the affluent, of fashion aficionados and of those seeking something special. The store is a place

of pilgrimage, a kind of open secret shared by shoppers with an eye for the exceptional. The interplay between past and present also appears in the windows, which often combine old-fashioned ideas – quintessential English tales, for example – with technological innovations. By introducing themes that reflect contemporary sensibilities, Harvey Nichols establishes a dialogue with passers-by that draws on current cultural moods. 'We try to interact, to get people to feel that they are having a conversation, that they are part of the gang,' says Wardley.

She and her team follow a number of subtle codes to engage the many eyes drawn to their windows. Viewers observe their work from various vantage points and in various states of mind. Leisurely strolling passers-by, sullen drivers stuck in traffic, tourists travelling by coach from airport to hotel, taxi drivers, cyclists whizzing past – each glances at the window display in a different way. The story they see there communicates on multiple levels to an audience composed of highly diverse elements. 'A lot of the people sitting at the traffic lights look

across at the windows,' says Wardley. 'People in cars and buses strain their necks to see the windows. The windows are something that people go out

'There is actually the whole shop — the pavement in front, the trees outside, the road. There's no reason why you can't work with the whole area.'
Thomas Heatherwick

of their way to look at.' She goes on to mention not only the many layers of communication involved in their designs, but also the scale of the windows and the number of angles from which they can be viewed.

Heatherwick expands on the theme: 'The window is one tool that is available to you. But there is actually the whole shop – the pavement in front, the trees outside, the road. People are dying for interesting things to happen. There's no reason why you can't work with the whole area.'

FROM LEFT TO RIGHT
Max Mara on 2
Sheshanna on 3
Jimmy Choo Shoes on 1

Bernhard Willhelm on 1
Issey Miyake on 1g1
... March on 1g1
Poste Shoes on 1g1
Mens Accessories on 1g1

— May 2003: Responding to the change in season, the Summer Flowers window adds a touch of humour to Britain's characteristically unpredictable weather.

FROM LEFT TO RIGHT
D Squared
Dries van N...
Marc Jacobs
Poste Shoes
Mens Acces...

Clements R...
Swimwear on 3
Designer Shoes on...
Accessories on 3

Lynn ... Vintage on 1
Missoni Mara Swimwear on...
Accessories on 3
Designer Shoes on 1

— Installed by Icon Studios, in collaboration with Harvey Nichols' in-house display team, the Summer Flowers scene, with its petalled sun peeking out from behind the clouds create a childlike fantasy, imbued with optimism and fun.

Reuters/WFA

Berlin, Germany (1 May 2002). A looter leaves a Berlin Kreuzberg supermarket during fierce May-Day riots in this area of the city. Violence broke out on Wednesday in the wake of peaceful left-wing and anti-Nazi demonstrations.

Speaki
Lang

ng Sign
uage

Luxury, tradition and invention converge behind the windows at Maison Hermès in Tokyo, courtesy of an array of guest designers

HERMÈS

Speaking Sign Language

Text by KANAE HASEGAWA
Photography by
SATOSHI ASAKAWA

TOKYO — The alluring window displays of luxury-goods retailer Hermès Japan are a feast for the eyes. They can be enjoyed by both passers-by and the happy few who can actually afford to shop in such places. Window displays mirror our increasingly materialistic world in much the same way as advertisements do. And like ads, the presentations that line our streets are an important point of contact with potential customers. Considerable creativity is put into publicizing seasonal collections, especially at the top end of the retail market. Luxury retailers, in particular, have raised the window display to something of an art form. They give as much attention to their street presence as to any other vehicle of publicity.

Hermès Japan understands that the shop window is more than a platform for showcasing the latest bag or belt. The window forms an interface between fashion house and public. It communicates what the brand represents. Leila Menchari has been the

> *'Window displays reflect the dreams of society. They need to look contemporary, while also conveying the timeless, classic craftsmanship that goes into all our products.'*
> *Kozo Fujimoto*

sole creator of window displays at the Hermès store in Paris since 1977. But at Maison Hermès, the big Hermès outlet in Ginza, Tokyo, the retailer has worked with no fewer than ten international artists and designers on a series of rotating displays since the store opened in 2001. Designed by Renzo Piano, Maison Hermès is a serene ten-storey edifice wrapped almost entirely in blank façades of glass block. Inside, retail floors are topped by offices and, on the uppermost level,

— The Italian-glass-block façade of Renzo Piano's ten-storey Maison Hermès glows in the dark. Photography by Michel Denancé.

— In her design for a 2003 footwear display, Japanese artist Izumi Kon crafted backdrop, column and stool in Corian. Kon's acrylic painting of the shoes expresses a more personal view of the handmade products.

— Jasper Morrison borrowed historical Hermès product images for the wallpaper used in his 2003 display. These traditional items provide a subtle contrast to the Corian furnishings that draw Morrison's design into the here and now.

— A window display by graphic-design team Groovisions revolves around a giant Rolodex whose flip-over cards bear sign-language symbols, a clever reference to 'La Main', the Hermès theme for 2002. A second reference, seen in the background, is an enlarged image of the hand-shaped Kadena key holder.

A

dis-
mès
hey
and
ford
dis-
teri-
y as
the
are
with
able
sea-
top
re-
the
art
on to
ther

t the
form
belt.
be-
c. It
pre-
the

t the
But
rmès
has
nter-
on a
the
d by
is a
d al-
glass
ped
evel,

— Jon Kessler's 2002 mobile includes a cast-metal hand and foot welded to a steel pipe. Balancing the mobile is an ensemble of scarf, hat, jacket and glove.

— For the winter 2003 collection, Jon Kessler created a two-part display. In the first scene, a fur coat hangs on a sign suggesting sunnier climes. In the snowy scene that follows, Styrofoam reindeer discover an abandoned picnic set and a pair of gloves.

a small cinema. Though the store's two window displays are dwarfed beneath the huge expanse of glazing, they do overlook Ginza's main commercial thoroughfare, with its steady stream of shoppers, office workers and tourists passing by.

Exploiting this location to the full, Hermès has developed a coherent concept for window arrangements based on simple narratives that are easy to read yet always visually clever. A minuscule theatre, the Hermès win-

dow stages a single scene featuring a discreetly placed glove, shoe, briefcase or other item of coveted merchandise. Surrounding scenery affirms the brand's hallmarks of tradition and luxury, the attention to fine detailing and, above all, the aura of exclusiveness that characterizes the label.

'Window displays reflect the dreams of society. They need to look contemporary, while also conveying the timeless, classic craftsmanship that goes into all our products,' says Kozo

Fujimoto, the man in charge of communications for the fashion house in Japan. Rather than working with an in-house team of specialists, Hermès takes the riskier but often more rewarding approach of letting outsiders dream up décors. Each small set is the work of an invited artist or designer whom Fujimoto feels will not only highlight the exclusiveness of the products, but also adopt an open-minded attitude to commercial merchandising. 'We look for figures whose

ideas and work resonate with the company's unyielding pursuit of quality in design and sensitivity to trends,' he says.

His view underlines the success formula that has made the brand a byword for quality, tradition and innovation. Ever since the company broadened its scope of activity from harnesses and saddles, it has placed a premium on following and even instigating trends. Hermès was the first company to apply industrial zips to handmade leather bags and to factory-produce belts and watchstraps in leather.

The pioneering spirit that marries

tradition and innovation is what Hermès likes to emphasize in its window presentations. Thus calling on creatives whose work is anchored in

---

A minuscule theatre, the Hermès window stages a single scene featuring a discreetly placed glove, shoe, briefcase or other item of coveted merchandise

---

the here and now is a clever strategy. They bring a modern visual sensibility to a fashion house whose roots lie in the nineteenth century. They also support the retailer's entry into lucrative areas like perfumery, porcelain, glassware and silverware. The strategy of moving into new markets is about more than simply boosting sales. Glass-making and silversmithing are of interest to Hermès because these disciplines rely on the same excellence in craftsmanship that is at the core of the brand.

'Creating an inspiring display is very much a collaborative effort,' says Fujimoto. 'We want people who will

— I
aga
fine

— In a scene created by Japanese designer Tokujin Yoshioka, a swinging Hermès handbag alludes to the presence of a woman walking, and a moving saddle evokes the image of a galloping horse.

— This 2003 display by Satoshi Hirose features a blue acrylic light box and a clear glass table, indicating the endless depths of the sea.

— A world atlas printed on a wooden panel forms the backdrop for this 2001 window design by Groovisions. Handbags are displayed on wooden boxes covered in orange leather.

— In 2003, artist Tetsuya Nakamura took advantage of the display windows that flank the store entrance on two sides. The door to the shop is at the centre of his MDF luxury yacht. The background is a blow-up of the striped scarf featured in that season's Hermès collection.

work with us to unlock a new world.' His list of collaborators includes artist Jon Kessler and designers Tokujin Yoshioka (see *Frame* magazine, issue 27) and Jasper Morrison. Others are Satoshi Hirose, graphic artists Groovisions and lacquer specialist Tetsuya Nakamura.

Even though guest window-dressers are set to work with an annual 'concept theme', they enjoy a generous measure of latitude when it comes to artistic expression. Anything goes, as long as the display meets the impec-

cable standards set for the company's products. In 2001 Groovisions responded to the theme 'Looking for the Beauty of the Earth' with a stunning

Invited creatives bring a modern visual sensibility to a fashion house whose roots lie in the nineteenth century

map of the world based on the Goode Homolosine Projection and printed on large wooden panels interconnected with oversized zips. As the backdrop of the display, the map acknowledged the French firm's position set in the world-wide market. Draped casually on pedestals were a few seasonal items like a blanket and a hat. A year later the same designers created a display that revolved around 'La Main' (French for 'the hand'). A giant Rolodex in one window featured a sign-language symbol on each of its

flip-over cards. Displayed in the next window was the complete alphabet. Sandals and scarves illustrated the importance of handmade details. 'Sign language was an appropriate motif to reflect the craftsman's skilled hands,' says Hiroshi Ito of Groovisions. The graphically gesticulating hands – a reference to dexterity in design and to direct visual communication – succinctly symbolized the Hermès brand and the function of window display.

A 2003 display by Milan-based Japanese artist Satoshi Hirose was a natural extension of both the shop's merchandising campaign and his own art. Hirose expanded a 'Mediter-ranean' theme to include travel and memory. A dry desert landscape requiring 400 kilograms of sand appeared in one of two windows, where a pair of winter gloves and a briefcase looked as though they'd been casually discarded by a northerner in search of water. The second window held a box of transparent acrylic illuminated by blue light, suggesting the endless depths of the sea. Floating on the calm surface were a hat and a travel bag. The two scenes, scorching sand next to cool blue water, triggered images of a Mediterranean beach, while forming an imaginative backdrop for the travel accessories on display.

In winter 2003, New York-based artist Jon Kessler also played with the idea of reality versus fantasy, but in a more light-hearted vein to suit the festive season. Scene 1, in an arctic setting, depicted Santa's reindeers discovering an abandoned picnic set and a pair of gloves. In Scene 2, a fur coat hanging over a signpost pointed to three sunny destinations on the Cote d'Azur, a reminder of the previous summer's Mediterranean theme. Here, as in all Hermès displays, subtly placed products play a part in the painterly composition. Each designer uses such props to tell a story about the French *maison*.

— Three glass display cases set in a desert of sand present the 2003 Autumn/Winter Collection.

— In one of graphic-design team Groovisions' 'La Main' displays, items from the Spring/Summer Collection appear against a panel of sign-language symbols. Flanking the latest products by Hermès are boxes with blown-up images of finely crafted details illustrating the quality of the handwork.

Zurich, Switzerland. Rioters leave a broken display window at the Yves Saint Laurent boutique on Zurich's Bahnhofstrasse.

Courtesy of http://philip.greenspun.com. Photography by Philip Greenspun.

Ducks, Dio

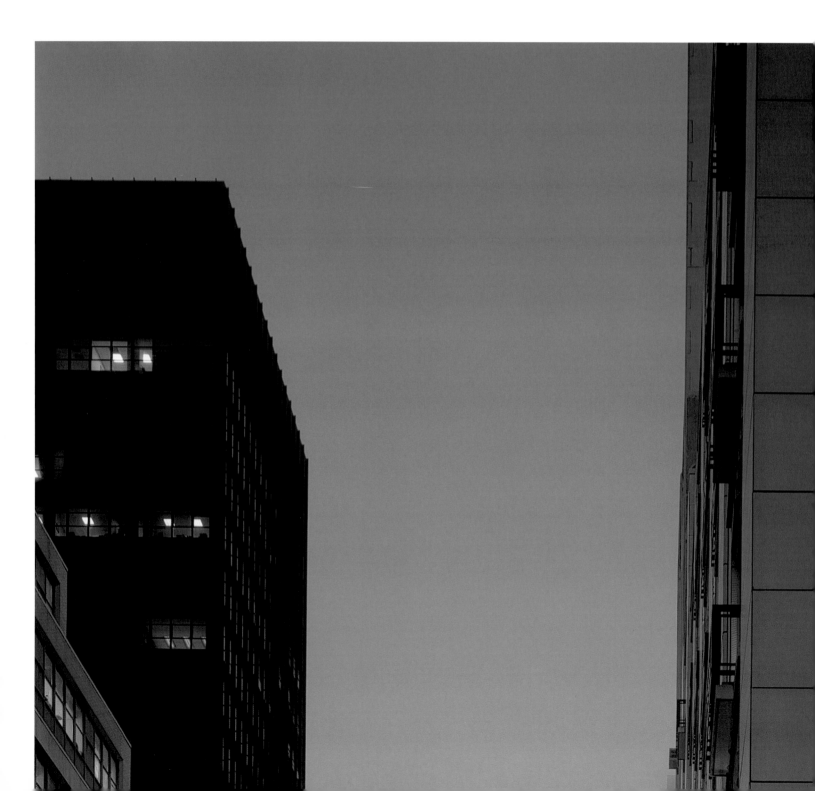

r and Dolly

Displaying an unmistakably British sense of humour, Simon Doonan's finest scenarios for luxury department store Barneys are expressive in their contrariness, appearing creepily banal or regally puerile

BARNEYS

uptight: rage, homophobia, the AIDS plague, celebrity. Sometimes the store

Ducks, Dior and Dolly

— Barneys boasts a prime location at the corner of Madison Avenue and 61st Street. Passers-by gape in admiration at window displays created by Simon Doonan's design team. Photography by Frank Oudeman.

**Text by SHONQUIS MORENO
Photography by ARI MESA**

NEW YORK — Born with a lisp into what he respectfully calls a 'family of lunatics', Simon Doonan blossomed in a suburban British household that included a lobotomized grandmother, a blind aunt living in the attic and an uncle with paranoid schizophrenia. By age ten, he knew he was a pouf. Today, Doonan's cheeky authenticity – in the form of window display for luxury department store Barneys – has become a New York City landmark. 'Doonan was instrumental in shifting the image of Barneys,' says Joseph Weishar, professor of display and exhibit design at New York's Fashion Institute of Technology. 'The image that he's projected has come out clearer than anything that the store has said about itself.'

Lisp gone, 52-year-old Doonan is aging handsomely. A larger-than-life character the size of a Royal Ascot jockey, for three decades he has created dioramas that occasionally cause a shriek to go up from the pavement. Calling himself a freak, as well as infantile and *outré*, Doonan peppers his speech with British slang like naff, wally and poncy, while using the flamboyant constructions of an urban queen – if it's not 'ultra-groovy', it's 'fab' – expressions that suggest a swoosh of the wrist. In person, how-

It is professionally risky to incorporate sex, religion or furry animals larger than mice into a window unless the objective is a certain grey-haired je ne sais quoi.

ever, he's down to earth and as candid as his work. 'Any twit can design windows,' he says without irony. 'Designing the windows, to me, is like watching television. It's very fun, and it's not particularly challenging. I've always had a provocative point of view and have wanted to do things that were attention-getting, not just pretty, and that's become a significant part of the Barneys identity – the luxurious product juxtaposed with the slightly irreverent window displays.' In 1986, the year that Barneys

hired Doonan, there was only one store downtown, the company had just begun to sell women's fashions, and his boss told Doonan he wanted to have the most interesting windows in the world. Today there are ten Barneys shops and 14 outlets around the globe, and Doonan is the creative force behind every window involved. By now, experience has taught him a few things: that it behoves one to collaborate with artists, to hire those smarter than oneself, to copy other people's ideas, to exaggerate one's shortcomings, and to cram perishable food, live ducks and starving art students into display windows. That it is entertain-

Some of Doonan's designs have an austere, documentary sense of composition, like a Diane Arbus photograph

ing to needle the politically correct and to fail utterly to take the fashion industry seriously. That it is, however, professionally risky to incorporate sex, religion or furry animals larger than mice into a window unless the objective is to give yourself a certain grey-haired *je ne sais quoi*.

Some of Doonan's designs have an austere, documentary sense of composition, like a Diane Arbus photograph. Others, seemingly doodled and unballasted, run amok. Each window is only the meme of an anecdote; Doonan rarely provides a whole narrative but manages, nonetheless, to evoke the fumes of a backstory. He combines opposing elements, such as gutted mattresses with Dior suits and trash with Chanel-clad ladies-who-lunch. His finest scenarios are expressive in their contrariness: They are creepily banal or regally puerile. In Doonan's world, ambiguity often muddles the everyday. Twilit back gardens and silent vacuum cleaners provide the settings and props for temper tantrums – the tantrums of grown-ups, not children. In one window, a mother mannequin pours tin after tin of lighter fluid onto a grill filled with blazing coals, blithely discarding the empties at her feet. Doonan has demonstrated his capacity to amplify or deflate anything that causes the culture around him to become shrill and

uptight: rage, homophobia, the AIDS plague, celebrity. Sometimes the store gets complaints: After Magic Johnson admitted he was HIV-positive, the basketball player's likeness appeared in a window beside, among many other objects, two small Christmas trees hung with gold-wrapped condoms. An uproar ensued. Often, however, the designer lowers the decibel by using our rubbish, laddered stockings, broken TV sets and celebrities to make us laugh. And you can't laugh at your celebrities without laughing at yourself.

Part of Doonan's appeal lies in an ability to laugh loudest at himself. His sense of humour is unmistakably British. He co-opts our most controversial icons – the things and people that stir up our emotions and through which we reveal both our weaknesses and our virtues – and reflects them back at us. He mixes high and pop culture in the same way he mixes images of what we fear (AIDS, anger) with what we wish for (sex, self-expression). One of the last times he used realistic mannequins was in 1989, when he says they began to look like

After Magic Johnson admitted he was HIV-positive, the basketball player's likeness appeared in a window that also featured two small Christmas trees hung with gold-wrapped condoms. An uproar ensued

characters out of a soap opera. In the mid-90s, as the fashion industry began to cultivate celebrity worship, Doonan collaborated with sculptor Martha King on a series of windows that both lauded and caricatured famous Americans like Madonna, Senator Jesse Helms (accompanied by reindeer named Homophobia, Racism and Bigotry) and Dolly Parton (105-centimetre bust, 88-centimetre waist). 'The Great Queens of England' windows curtseyed to Quentin Crisp, Alexander McQueen, and Manolo Blahnik. Holiday windows spoofed people as elves: Elfton John celebrated the season with Giself and Elf Saint Laurent. 'I'm not an elitist,' says Doonan. 'I don't like elitism in fashion – it's stupid and boring. I think that windows

— As shoes account for a good slice of the sales at Barneys, display staff regularly invent fresh ways to show them off. The simplicity and effectiveness of this 2002 solution is characteristic of Doonan's approach to design. He recalls the window as something that 'seemed like a silly thing to do'.

— A lesson that Doonan has learned well finds expression in this 1996 spring cleaning window: Most women who wear Rei Kawakubo's fashions never pick up a mop. The vast majority of people ogling Doonan's windows, however, are not Comme des Garçons customers. Is the joke on Barneys' shoppers or its window-shoppers? Surely a little of both.

— Successful window-display sight gags – like this 1995 skiing mishap – speak for themselves. Designed by Doonan in collaboration with Steven Johanknecht, this tragicomedy was crafted out of chicken wire and upholstery batting.

— Doonan says he's made found-object hearts 'about 20 times in different incarnations'. In the 1970s, for Maxfield's in Los Angeles, he crammed rubbish found on the street into wire frames. By 1997 he was making hearts out of boxing gloves and ductwork.

RICK OWE[...]

[...]ME NATIONAL

[...]AS FOU[...]

— This page and next page top left: Although lovely lighting and fine fashion complement the scene, artist Jocelyn Shipley's horned rubber headdresses are the stars of this 2003 display. 'Collaborating with artists', says Doonan, 'is one of the more interesting aspects of the job.'

— 'This is a Cocteau moment,' says Doonan of his surreal 2002 design featuring bodiless arms bearing handbags. 'Jean Cocteau opens an accessory boutique.'

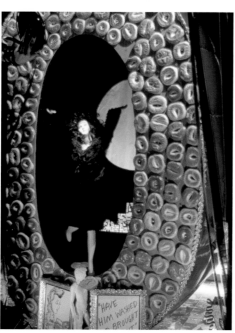

— To add sparkle to the 2003 holiday season, Doonan reprised his celebrity caricatures with a take on Cher, asking sculptor Martha King to create a Cher for every decade. Doonan came up with the tagline: 'The holidays are for Cher-ing.'

are a very low common denominator, and they should communicate to people.'

After graduating from Manchester University in 1972 with a degree in psychology and art history, Doonan worked at Aquascutum, Turnbull & Asser and at Nutter's, a shop on Savile Row, before emigrating to the United States in 1978 to dress the windows of Los Angeles department store Maxfield. Doonan beckoned to Maxfield's sardonic rock-star clientele with mannequins lounging in coffins and mangy coyotes abducting hipsters' babies. Eight years on, at Barneys, Doonan began to pile and hang merchandise with studied sloppiness or obsessive, Warholian repetition. The product itself became the prop. He commissioned the work of influential downtown artists, sometimes collaborating with them. He constructed sculptures from tights, floors from Chinese chequerboards, foggy scenes from grease-rubbed glass, valentine hearts out of ductwork or boxing

'I don't like elitism in fashion — it's stupid and boring.'
Simon Doonan

gloves. He draped the windows with reams of orange plastic roadworks fencing, Astroturf, 13,000 Q-tips, blue plastic flyswatters, rolls of toilet paper and, in one case, 68 boxes of shellacked pink wafers. Inspired by the boom of American reality television in 2001, Doonan created a window for each decade from the 1940s through the 1980s, inhabited at peak traffic hours by live occupants clad in period costume (two female fashion students, one in drag): Twiggy paired with Keith Moon, Ivana with Donald Trump. Pedestrians voted for what Doonan called 'the grooviest couple'; the prize was a US$2000 scholarship.

Doonan's window display is a skilful combination of design and craft, though he compares it to a 'hokey' form of packaging design. 'The key,' he says, 'is to take everything unbelievably seriously and not seriously at the same time. I'm maniacally driven, but if something doesn't work out, I can let go of it. I can't waste a morning having a big mood swing about something that didn't work out exactly the way I wanted it to. I'd rather just get on with something else.'

— Square sheep made of Styrofoam packing peanuts are joined by a bird on the wing crafted of bubble wrap and cardboard tubes – all materials found in the studio. 'It's very, very low tech,' says Doonan of the 1998 window, admitting that he's fond of the result produced by 'the ratty, found-object quality of the props contrasting with the refinement of the clothing'.

— Mimicking the new 'infantile art' coming out of Britain in 1998, Doonan and his team came up with their own interpretation of Sarah Lucas's 'tights' sculptures. He says the work was inspired by the Sensation art exhibition, a show that did indeed cause a sensation in New York City that year.

Floor

— Another Doonan secret: The simpler the props, the better. In 2002, candy wrappers attached to strings hanging from the ceiling gave this display the spirit of an art installation – or a very heart-warming downpour. Doonan has used fly swatters in a similar way.

HAPPY HOLIDAYS 1940

— Previous page bottom right and this spread: in 2000, Doonan designed period-piece windows for various decades of the twentieth century. During peak traffic hours, he animated the scenes with costumed couples (both women, one in drag). Passers-by voted for the 'grooviest' couple and the girls – all art students – walked away with a US$2000 scholarship.

— In October 2003, original costumes from *The Last Samurai*, designed by Ngila Dickson, appear together with contemporary Western attire. In the foreground, a still from the film features actors in the same costumes.

Practical

IQUIS MORENO
y by **JEREMY CHU**

Over 200 years ago,
p & Low opened its
n. Although today the
oldest retail store in
esents a fresh face, si-
nostalgic and modern:
isual Display Director
uwman's finely crafted
y imagined window de-

blocks, coloured pencils,
and moss. 'She's imagina
the-beaten-path,' says r
Martin Pegler, who taugh
for a year at New York Ci
Institute of Technology
cluded her work in book:
thored since. 'She uses m
are mundane, trite, ord
makes them different, cr

This past spring, Bouw
Shreve's windows in silk
series of jewel-box garde
pastoral scenes, cut-cry

Magic

en grass
e and off-
il expert
ouwman
s Fashion
l has in-
e has au-
rials that
ry – but
ve.'

n dressed
create a
In these
goblets

sheep; and each 'sky' was filled with a miniature Tord Boontje-designed chandelier – a frothy, light-filled tangle of cut-metal flowers. Bouwman gives the window a secret life. Her scenes feel conjured but not contrived: It's easy to imagine that just beyond the sill lies a rolling landscape of lollipop trees and ponds brimming with clotted cream – passers-by are granted a glimpse of fairyland. 'I don't want the window displays to look traditional,' says Bouwman. 'A great window should stop us from just hurrying

Lucy-Ann Bouwman's windows for Boston retailer Shreve, Crump & Low underscore the pervasive presence of enchantment in everyday life

SHREVE, CRUMP & LOW

agic

— The reopening in October 2002 of the Boston Ritz Carlton inspired Lucy-Ann Bouwman's plush re-creations of the hotel's interior, including a chic doll's-house chandelier and the narrowing perspective down a carpeted, white-laminate corridor. Amethyst, amber and diamond rings are on display.

— February 2003: Referring to love letters written with a quill pen, a variation on the Peter-Pan-Loves-Wendy theme, and to the uplifting feelings evoked by love, Bouwman places jewellery on a bed of feathers. The red feather from Peter Pan's cap stands for love.

— June 2004: Shreve's intimate shadow-box display windows are found at the corner of Boylston and Arlington Streets. Although the jeweller is the oldest retailer in America, the store presents an eternally fresh face to passers-by. Working with small windows requires Bouwman to design at an unfamiliar scale, says retail expert Martin Pegler: 'You're looking, like Alice, through the keyhole.' Photography by Chris Akelian.

Practical Magic

By SHONQUIS MORENO
Photography by JEREMY CHU

BOSTON — Over 200 years ago, Shreve, Crump & Low opened its doors to Boston. Although today the jeweller is the oldest retail store in America, it presents a fresh face, simultaneously nostalgic and modern: the result of Visual Display Director Lucy-Ann Bouwman's finely crafted and effortlessly imagined window design.

Like a collector assembling a cabinet of curiosities, Bouwman composes uncommon dioramas using common objects: eggs, children's building blocks, coloured pencils, even grass and moss. 'She's imaginative and off-the-beaten-path,' says retail expert Martin Pegler, who taught Bouwman for a year at New York City's Fashion Institute of Technology and has included her work in books he has authored since. 'She uses materials that are mundane, trite, ordinary – but makes them different, creative.'

This past spring, Bouwman dressed Shreve's windows in silk to create a series of jewel-box gardens. In these pastoral scenes, cut-crystal goblets and decanters hovered midair like dragonflies; foam floral spheres covered with moss and straw were crowned with bracelets and necklaces as if to suggest plump, jewel-eyed sheep; and each 'sky' was filled with a miniature Tord Boontje-designed chandelier – a frothy, light-filled tangle of cut-metal flowers. Bouwman gives the window a secret life. Her scenes feel conjured but not contrived: It's easy to imagine that just beyond the sill lies a rolling landscape of lollipop trees and ponds brimming with clotted cream – passers-by are granted a glimpse of fairyland. 'I don't want the window displays to look traditional,' says Bouwman. 'A great window should stop us from just hurrying by.' When jewellery is presented as mere merchandise it becomes just that – more stuff. Bouwman hopes her windows will 'create an experience and become part of someone's memory.

f the
hite-

— September 2003: The end of summer inspires Bouwman's use of antique wooden doll's desks to usher in the school year. Passers-by are invited to read and observe the miniature objects on the desks: tiny notebooks, a mini atlas and written notes. Jewellery becomes part of the magical discovery of display: a ruby horseshoe for good luck and an American-flag brooch on the satchel.

Ultimately, they're supposed to be magical, places where one looks through a scrim of fantasy.' These windows do much more than support the product. They make the product part of an image or a narrative larger than itself. The moral of the story? Experiences, more than pretty presentations, sell stuff.

Everything and nothing is exotic to Bouwman, who was born in Beirut, studied fashion merchandising in Toronto and display and exhibit design in New York, and who, since the autumn of 2001, has divided her time between Amsterdam and Boston. Among her influences, she counts her father, a Dutch jazz musician, and her mother, a Lebanese nursery-school teacher. Her windows combine expert craftsmanship with blue notes and the paste-pot-and-round-edged-scissors feeling of a kindergarten classroom. The comfort, delight and wonder evoked in Shreve's windows are Bouwman's own. She often uses materials as simple as shrubbery, metres of shantung or film celluloid, but she uses them in such a way as to inspire in viewers the same dilating sense of wonder that they experienced at seven, discovering something for the first time – an eclipse of the moon, the rushing sound inside a seashell. For the 2004/2005 holiday windows, she is planning to create a series of window-

— Part of a tribute to classics during the 2003 holiday season, an animated television programme starring Rudolph the Red-Nosed Reindeer plays in loops, allowing unhurried pedestrians to take in the whole show.

size kaleidoscopes made of mirrored tiles, crystals, fibre optics, LED lighting and lenticular vinyl. Each will spin automatically, as if someone were turning it slowly by hand.

'When I think of Lucy's windows, I remember musical notes and ballet slippers, and a Christmas tree made of artists' paint brushes with their tips dipped in paint,' says Tom Beebe,

once a window designer for Paul Stuart and currently fashion creative director at Daily News Record. Beebe met Bouwman in the mid-'90s, at a time when she was working under win-

— The 2003 winter-holiday windows pay tribute to American film classics, movies shown year after year during the country's most festive season. Featured here is a Charlie Chaplin comedy, *Gold Rush*, an appropriate partner for the sparkling array of gold and diamonds. Jewellery is displayed on small film cans caught in an elegant snowdrift. The starry sky has fibre optics to thank for its glitter.

— February 2004: A bird's-eye perspective of lunch-for-two features fine porcelain, including teacups and teapot. Flowers at the centre of the table are cut-metal creations by Tord Boontje.

— A larger window offers the viewer a bird's-eye-perspective of a scene, positioned perpendicular to the window, that showcases a table laid with dozens of fine porcelain dinner plates. In the centre, a plate bearing the word 'art' not only calls attention to the palette of colours, but also cheekily labels the display itself.

— April 2003: To mark an event in Boston called Edible Art, Bouwman recruited Denise Ortakales, illustrator of children's books, to create paper sculptures of 'gems people eat'. Works of art include paper chocolates, pasta and sandwiches piled high with crisps.

dow legend Gene Moore. 'Lucy keeps the craft in windows but gives them a modern spin. The result is windows and design ideas that make people think.'

Shreve's 17 windows undergo a transformation every six weeks. Installation, with the help of several freelancers, takes at least 12 hours. Bouwman has worked with large windows

Lucy-Ann Bouwman hopes her windows will 'create an experience and become part of someone's memory. Ultimately, they're supposed to be magical, places where one looks through a scrim of fantasy'

like those at Bergdorf Goodman, where she freelanced in the mid-'90s, but, like Moore before her, she usually works with smaller windows, called 'shadow boxes' – those at Shreve, for instance, are 44.45 x 60.04 x 58.42 cm when seen from the street. Shadow boxes often serve as the face of high-end shops like Hermès, Bulgari, Birks and Estée Lauder, for whom Bouwman has also worked. The limited size of the shadow box, however, means that she must translate her ideas and props into dollhouse dimensions. 'When you're working with large windows, you're working with life-size

material,' says Pegler, 'but in a shadow box, you're working in a very limited space. You have to adapt life-size things to a miniature scale. You're looking, like Alice, through the keyhole, at a different perspective of things. Lucy-Ann really has to take that potion and miniaturize herself to get into what she's working on.'

Since 1991, Bouwman has designed displays on a monthly basis for Kenneth's Hair Salon at the Waldorf Astoria Hotel, creating mannequin heads coiffed with surreal hairstyles made from shells, hatpins, feathers, tiny terracotta flower pots, or even fortune cookies. She is inspired by the everyday, but she seems to view it lavishly, romantically, and with great optimism. Her February 2003 Valentine's windows honoured the real-life love between two people whom she depicted as Peter Pan and Wendy. By papering the rear of each window with the cut-out silhouette of a scene, she illustrated the tiny, telling, domestic details – Wendy darning Peter's shadow onto his feet – that make a legendary romance. The 2002 holiday windows told a story about wishing on a star and featured sparkling Art-Deco figures, made of model-maker's sculpting foam, reclining in the cradle of a crescent moon. 'Those windows captured the idea of looking far into the heavens, to infinity, and dreaming,' says Bouwman. 'When I designed them, I was thinking about when I was little. I used to play on a swing and try to swing really hard and

high because I wanted to touch the sky.'

In another window, leafless winter trees clad in mirrored tiles instead of bark reflected rainbows onto a dark sky (the rear wall), while delicate teacups too shelter from the storm inside the bare frames of teensy houses. In this way – mixed into an otherworldly landscape, placed unobtrusively to the side of the window or slightly obscured behind a coat of Lumisty film so that its outlines are softened through the glass – Shreve's merchandise becomes the embellishment instead of the props. Bouwman makes the product feel remote and proximate at the same time: a ring exists some-

Bouwman makes the product feel remote and proximate at the same time: a ring exists someplace closer to us and yet worshipfully far — in our mind's eye. And isn't that the best way to sustain desire?

place closer to us and yet worshipfully far — in our mind's eye. And isn't that the best way to sustain desire? This is the essential 'magic' of Bouwman's windows: they underscore the pervasive presence of enchantment in everyday life. They suggest that magic is a real thing.

— Bouwman and Jonathan Ro-Schofield designed a series of bicycle-themed windows in observance of American Independence Day (July 2004). They used every part of the bike, from handlebars (complete with an old-fashioned bell) and a wicker basket to an automatically rotating pedal and wheel. The designers opted for the components of full-size bicycles, fitting their choices into the available space. The window not only underlines a contradiction in proportion, but also creates a link between the jewellery on display and the components of a bicycle. Photography by Chris Akelian.

— Wendy darns Peter Pan's shadow to his feet in a series of Valentine's Day 2003 windows that use laser-cut polystyrene silhouettes to celebrate the mundane details of a fabled love. Displays are designed as three-layered stage sets: proscenium (needle and thread), centre stage (silhouette of Wendy and Peter Pan) and front stage (diamond heart pendant).

Reuters/WFA

Buenos Aires, Argentina (21 December 2001). Shop owners stand in their ransacked shop in Buenos Aires. Argentine President Fernando de la Rua resigned amid the worst civil unrest in more than a decade. Protesters, furious at deepening austerity and poverty, continued to loot well into the night, raising the nationwide death toll to 25.

It's the p
that

roducts

ount

By DAVID LIT
Photograp
EROS BE

NEW YORK, PARIS
the centre of an imma
is the skull of a water

GUCCI

Working instinctively, John Field creates carefully controlled, sinister and sometimes even threatening spaces inhabited by the Gucci brand

GUCCI

It's the products that count

— Autumn/Winter 2002: A figure stands against a hand-painted background depicting a moody sky, out of which approaches a swirling mass of undefined creatures. The mannequin is either blissfully unaware of the spectacle, or is standing resolutely against it.

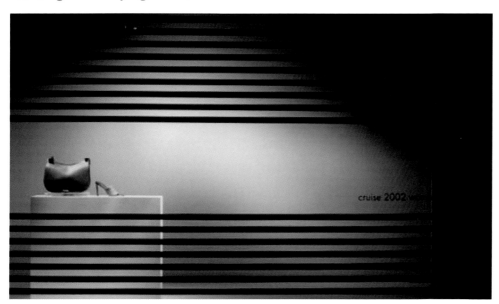

— Spring/Summer 2002: Simple, sleek objects (handbag and shoe) are placed off-centre within a restricted field of view. Horizontal black lines that correspond to the simple geometries of the objects have been applied directly to the window glass. A display of careful composition.

By DAVID LITTLEFIELD
Photography by
EROS BESCHI

NEW YORK, PARIS — Staring from the centre of an immaculate white wall is the skull of a water buffalo with outrageously large horns. An arresting object, it demonstrates the power of the unexpected, of the out of scale. It is so out of place as to be almost ridiculous. This is John Field's office.

Field is Gucci's window designer.

Rather than obliterating shadow, John Field cultivates it to squeeze every drop of drama out of his materials

He is a direct, honest, unaffected man with an exceptional eye for detail and a highly developed sense of the surreal. He is one of those designers to whom ideas seem to come naturally and inevitably. He resists theoretical interpretations of his work, which is probably wise; he works too fast to pause and ask what his creations actually mean. And his stage sets are too visually rich and suggestive to be the result of purely rational thought. Field begins with the glimmer of an idea, and two weeks later the set is complete – mannequins set against a wall of candy or a background of feathers, figures accompanied by a hooded bird. He is instinctive, a man strong on impulse without being impulsive.

Field's instinctive approach is partially explained by the lack of a formal education. Having left school in Birmingham, England, at 16, he soon found himself working on window displays at Rackhams department store. Luckily, Field thrived on this unplanned career, soon leaving for London where

— Spring/Summer 2004: John Field employed rows of imitation candyfloss as a background for this collection. Arranged along a grid of diagonals, fashions stand out against a substance of the utmost sweetness, fragility and delicacy – but one which withers to nothing over time.

— Spring/Summer 2002: A denim collection is displayed against a textured backdrop covered in a coat of thickly applied black/blue paint. Virtually all colour has been drained from the scene, allowing pure contrast to lend the setting its power.

— Spring/Summer 2004: Tom Ford's press release for this collection referred to the runway models as 'arm candy'. Field responded by placing the mannequins against a backdrop of candy-filled Plexiglas boxes. The intensity of the lighting grows as natural light fades.

— Spring/Summer 2004: Assembled for the retrospective of one decade of Tom Ford's collections, a series of mannequins gather before an illuminated backdrop that bears the repeated phrase, 'Tom Ford for Gucci'. This was a difficult project; summing up Ford's collections in one simple, effective gesture was one of Field's more challenging briefs. The use of text, unusual in Field's work, provided the solution.

*from
wall
out-
sting
er of
le. It
dicu-
gner.*

*tes
of
ds*

*man
and
sur-
rs to
rally
etical
ch is
st to
s ac-
e too
e the
Field
, and
plete
all of
hers,
bird.
g on
.
par-
rmal
Birm-
ound
olays
uck-
nned*

— Spring/Summer 2002: Here Field has placed simple, sleek handbags and shoes off-centre within a restricted field of view. Applied to the glass are horizontal black lines that complement the spare design of the accessories. The

— Spring/Summer 2004: John Field's reflective boxes present accessories in an almost casual manner. Like many of his projects, this display emerges from an intuitive response; the significance of the scenario is not planned in advance,

careful composition reduces large windows to focused slots, thus allowing a careful handling of light, which reinforces the minimal displays.

but lies in an examination of the finished work. We see the merchandise displayed haphazardly in a series of colourful niches. Each is viewed both independently and as part of a family.

196

— Autumn/Winter 2002: An atmospheric background and a hooded eagle provide the setting for the Gothic collection: a striking scene that evokes a sense of danger, control, balance and poise.

— Autumn/Winter 2002: Gucci's Gothic collection inspired one of Field's more sinister creations, which features hooded birds, moody backgrounds and images of destruction. The birds, suggestive of falconry, lend the displays a peculiar blend of sophistication and danger clearly seen in this image, in which a large and perhaps malevolent bird sits comfortably on the arm of a woman in white.

only when strictly necessary. Another critical element is lighting, which is often the result of a gut feeling and experimentation. In most cases, Field illuminates his work with a single light source or from a single direction. Rather than obliterating shadow, he cultivates it to squeeze every drop of drama out of his materials. The feathers that formed the background of his 2003 spring/summer display were lit so obliquely that their shadow had more of a presence than the feathers themselves. In other displays, he has used lighting to pick out selected elements – a gloved hand or a row of buttons – leaving shadows to throw a seam or crease into sharp relief.

Although Field has been working exclusively for Gucci since 2003, he has had a relationship with the fashion house since 1990. The success of the partnership rests on a threefold foundation. To begin with, Gucci has a short chain of command, which means that Field receives rapid feed-

'A lot of Gucci is hard-edged and angular,' says Field, adding that the fashions have a strong linearity that is 'formal and very clear'

back on his sketch designs. Then, too, the fashion house is prepared to entertain Field's flights of fancy and contextual associations. (In the 1990s, he set Gucci's product range against a backdrop of Tabasco bottles and packets of Sweet'N Low, purely for the colour match; and an Easter display in 2004 featured boiled sweets set in resin – Field's literal interpretation of women as 'arm candy'.) Lastly, Field's design instincts seem to coincide with a certain uncompromising angularity characteristic of Gucci products. 'A lot of Gucci is hard-edged and angular,' he says, adding that the fashions have a strong linearity that is 'formal and very clear'.

The benefit of the close association between Field and his client is obvious in the presentation of Gucci's Gothic collection, creations introduced in autumn/winter 2002. The menswear selection is displayed against a neutral background and accompanied by a single prop. But what a prop! Demanding respect and

he picked up work at places like Aquascutum and Lilywhites. By the age of 21 he was self-employed, as he has been ever since. During his informal apprenticeship, Field learned what he calls 'the trade': the art of stopping someone in the street and captivating them for a second or two, of drawing a pedestrian's eye to a specific object, of creating a context loaded with association. Field sums it

up as 'the aggressive visual attack'.

His tricks of 'the trade' are few in number, but effective. Field sees his art poised at some point on a continuum that includes architecture, interior design and set design. What he crafts are carefully controlled, artfully composed, three-dimensional spaces inhabited by the Gucci brand. His windows have considerable depth and texture; colour makes an appearance

— Spring/Summer 2003: Holes drilled into Plexiglas panels hold feathers, which create unique geometric patterns in this experimental display. Heightening the effect is dramatic lighting, which creates an ambiguity of soft versus sharp. Although the lighting is carefully controlled, the unpredictable behaviour of the feathers gives the display a life of its own.

— Spring/Summer 2003: Hundreds of imitation, spring-mounted butterflies – in hues geared to those of the collection – shimmer and provide a hint of movement. The popular image of the butterfly as something pure, carefree, delicate and delightful provides a perfect accompaniment to warm-weather apparel.

— Above and left: Spring/Summer 2003: A collection that recalls the '70s harmonizes with its swirling, feel-good background. Colours highlighted in the collection are picked up in the display. A striking three-dimensional graphic of simplicity, depth and compositional balance.

— Autumn/Winter 2002: Another example of the Gothic collection features a male figure and a powerful bird that appear relaxed in each other's company. The fashions on display seem to pop out of this rich environment of intense colour, depth and shadow.

of the display, however, you are constantly brought back to the simplicity of the figure. The design uses the same device that compels a guy to look a woman up and down.

John Field is a man of singular humility. He underplays the power of his own work, just as he is unmoved by the ego and razzmatazz of the fashion industry. He describes himself as a

---

The design uses the same device that compels a guy to look a woman up and down

---

'scribbler' and declares that contemporary art and photography provide him with inspiration 'for no particular reason'. He just likes them. Field is a man who says he enjoys running and later lets it slip that, at 51, he's run both the London and New York marathons in the last year. In the same way, he is comfortable with his place and doesn't entertain the idea of committing the cardinal sin of upstaging the clothes. 'It's the clothes that count,' he says. 'That's what really matters. What we do is just peripheral support.'

— Autumn/Winter 2002: As well as featuring figurines of eagles, the Gothic collection includes a series of large apocalyptic images in sepia tints. Presenting two objects against a vision of such awesome power not only adds to their allure, but also contrasts the craft of the fashion industry with the frightening effects of Nature. Apart from the volcano, Field defines the collection with images of a storm, lightning and demolition.

---

attention is a rather large, hooded eagle. Like most of Field's work, this window display defies a single reading. While embodying something outrageous, sinister and threatening, the stately bird of prey also radiates a sense of control, balance and poise. The scene carries the suggestion of falconry. Careful lighting illuminates the actors in this drama, who glow against a wall of multiple shadows. The entire ensemble conjures up the spirit of Goth, seemingly without much effort.

Field also has a knack for focusing the observer's attention on the human

figure in spite of the action going on elsewhere. Take the female mannequin clothed in a simple, figure-hugging dress and positioned against a background of elaborate pink swirls, a design for spring 2003. The collection that season, says Field, was unusual in that it contained 'multiple references' drawn from various decades and sources, including Japan. The folds, tones and asymmetric swellings of Field's ribbon provide an environment that appears to be on the move – it's impossible to look at this tableau without letting your eyes roam all over it. Even while absorbing every aspect

— Spring/Summer 2003: Here Field placed a Japanese-inspired collection against a backdrop of prints by eighteenth-century artist Kitagawa Utamaro. Late in his life, Utamaro concentrated on female portraiture, often choosing his models from the 'pleasure district'. This creation generates an air of nonchalance within a setting of sensuality.

— Spring/Summer 2003: Another example from the Japan-inspired collection. Against the work of eighteenth-century artist Kitagawa Utamaro, a mannequin seems to stand at the crossroads between East and West.

— Spring/Summer 2004: The lighting warms up this display as night descends. Elaborating on Tom Ford's remark that runway models are no more than 'arm candy', Field positioned mannequins against pastel strips of candy-filled boxes.

— Spring/Summer 2003: In this extraordinary display, Field envelops the mannequin in hundreds of imitation, spring-mounted butterflies, in shades that correspond to the collection. The result is a delightful burst of colour that shimmers, suggesting movement.

London, UK (1 May 2002). Proprietors of high-end boutiques in Mayfair – the area targeted by anti-capitalist protesters for their May-Day demonstrations – opt for protective barriers to safeguard their pricey merchandise, shield their windows and ward off the angry crowd.

Courtesy of Immoklink.com. Photography by Immo Klink. From the series Mayday at Mayfair, 'Prada', 2002. Lamdaprint on aluminium, 180 x 120 cm.

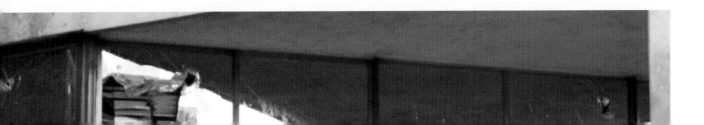

London, UK (1 May 2002). Mayfair is declared the official battleground for anticapitalist protests. Protective palisades hastily cover the display windows of London's most exclusive boutiques. In an

irony of fate, brands – effectively acting as their own censors – hide their products from the eyes of passers-by.

Mor
prot
25 tr
and

FOREFRONT

Index

Index

PHOTOGRAPHERS

PUBLI
FRAM
WWW.
BIRKH
Publi
archit
WWW.

COMP
The e
Frame

INTRO
Shonc

© 200
© 200

A CIP
Librar

Biblio
Biblio
Die D
Deutse
is avai

Copyr
writte

Brandscaping
Worlds of experience
in retail design
Otto Riewoldt (Ed.)

2002. 120 pages
100 colour, 13 b/w ills
and 34 drawings
24 x 22 cm. Softcover
ISBN 3-7643-6674-5
German / English

Brandscaping – the creation of
a three-dimensional brand
landscape – is increasingly
becoming central to the architecture of retail areas, shopping centres, and showrooms.
Architects and designers draw
on new technology and features from the entertainment
industry, answering the challenge of E-commerce and global
competition by staging encoun-
ters with the product as an
object of desire and sensual
experience.
Brandscaping presents 15 international projects ranging from
standard shop systems to
monumental theme parks,
including Volkswagen
AutoStadt, Wolfsburg,
Niketown in London, the City
Mall Sevens, Düsseldorf, the
shopping centre at Leipzig rail-
way station, the Showroom
Qiora New York, the shop concept Superga in Italy and the
Migros supermarket chain in
Switzerland. Concluding the
volume is a documentation of
discussions which took place
between image designers,
architects and interior architects during a related workshop.

PowerShop
New Japanese Retail Design
Carolien van Tilburg

2002. 224 pages
100 colour ills
29.7 x 23 cm. Hardcover
ISBN 3-7643-6626-5 English
In cooperation with Frame

Nowhere in the world does the
interior design of a shop
influence sales as it does in
Japan. Retailers spare no trou-
ble or expense when planning
and realising the design or
renovation of their premises.
PowerShop presents the best
and most recent retail designs
by ten Japanese interior architects. Shops and showrooms
created for established names
like Issey Miyake, Yohji
Yamamoto and Nissan share
centre stage with numerous
smaller, cutting-edge boutiques.
The designers presented here
prove that a shop can resemble
an art installation and still be
successful. They prove that it
pays to invest in creativity. And
they certainly prove that in
Japan imagination reigns.

Animation

Form Follows Fun
Regina Dahmen-Ingenhoven

2004. 359 pages
234 colour, 15 b/w ills
23.5 x 27 cm
Softcover with flaps
ISBN 3-7643-6631-1 English
ISBN 3-7643-6633-8 German

In amusement parks and theme parks the role of architecture in generating an emotional experience has long outgrown its mere functional and structural aspects. This trend is now pervading shopping malls, airports, museums, even banks, and is one which progressive architects will have to confront, as it becomes an increasingly important feature for investors and users in our pleasure-seeking society. With a wealth of international examples ranging from the prototype Disneyland (where Walt Disney's concepts of animation were congenially transformed into reality) to historical amusement parks and modern day theme parks, *Animation* investigates this global trend in contemporary architecture for the first time. Rich visual images and astute analytical texts reveal how animation architecture functions, the effects it can achieve and the uses it can be put to.

Wonderwall - Masamichi Katayama Projects

Frame Monographs of Contemporary Interior Architects

2003. 256 pages. 290 colour ills
23 x 29.7 cm. Hardcover
ISBN 3-7643-6954-X English
In cooperation with Frame

Unworldly spaces with equally unworldly names, like the topsy-turvy boutique And A, Beams T or Foot Soldier, shops that feature little conveyor belts for the display of merchandise, or Nowhere *A Bathing Ape 'Busy Work Shop', a Tokyo boutique that stocks and displays garments in an oversized refrigerator that resembles the familiar unit in everybody's local supermarket – all recent additions to Japan's shopping streets – are the work of Masamichi Katayama, founder of Tokyo-based WonderWall. More than just attempts to be futuristic or extravagant, they are highly sophisticated retail outlets. Not to mention great fun! Katayama is the consummate consumer. With his shop designs for *A Bathing Ape, a charismatic apparel brand, Katayama has ventured beyond the streets of Japan to enrich shopping experience in London and New York.

BIRKHÄUSER ⱽ/ₐ

**Birkhäuser –
Publishers for
Architecture**

Birkhäuser Publishers Ltd.
P.O. Box 133
CH-4010 Basel / Switzerland
Phone +41 61 2050-707
Fax +41 61 2050-792
e-mail: sales@birkhauser.ch
www.birkhauser.ch

FOREFRONT

THE CULTURE OF SHOPWINDOW DESIGN

PUBLISHERS
FRAME PUBLISHERS
www.framemag.com
BIRKHÄUSER –
Publishers for
architecture
www.birkhauser.ch

COMPILED BY
The editors of
Frame magazine

INTRODUCTION BY
Shonquis Moreno

CONTRIBUTIONS BY
Remi Abbas,
Kanae Hasegawa,
David Littlefield,
Sarah Martín Pearson,
Shonquis Moreno,
Chris Scott and
Charlotte Vaudrey

GRAPHIC DESIGN
Thomas Buxó

COPY EDITING
Donna de Vries-
Hermansader

TRANSLATION
InOtherWords: Donna de
Vries-Hermansader

COLOUR REPRODUCTION
Graphic Link,
the Netherlands
PRINTING
Rehms Druck,
Germany

DISTRIBUTION
Benelux, China, Japan,
Korea and Taiwan
ISBN 90-77174-08-7
Frame Publishers
Lijnbaansgracht 87
1015 GZ Amsterdam
the Netherlands
www.framemag.com

All other countries
ISBN 3-7643-7192-7
Birkhäuser – Publishers
for Architecture
PO Box 133
4010 Basel
Switzerland
Part of Springer Science
+Business Media
www.birkhauser.ch